D0174703

Praise for *Game-Based Marketing*

"The power of games to affect consumer behavior is almost limitless—and examples of powerful social games are all around us. *Game-Based Marketing* is the first look at combining the power of games with the power of marketing to create an exciting new user paradigm: Funware. This is clearly the future."

—Joel Brodie, CEO and Founder, Gamezebo.com

"Games are busting out of their traditional borders. No one knows that better than Gabe Zichermann who hit upon the insight early on that everybody, not just game makers, should use gamelike tricks to enthrall fans."

—Dean Takahashi, Editor of *VentureBeat*

"If you think games have already taken over the living room, wait until you see what they can do to advertising. Co-writers Zichermann and Linder have put forth cutting edge concepts about the power of game design in nongaming contexts. And you get five Achievement points if you read this endorsement."

— Bing Gordon, Venture Partner:
KPCB and Former CCO of Electronic Arts

"The rise of the multibillion dollar gaming industry demonstrates the appeal that compelling, interactive content has over other more passive forms of marketing. Zichermann, a [visionary] in the field of gaming and the application of gaming techniques, and co-writer Linder set forth in writing for the first time an actionable treatise on how smart brands can leverage what the gaming industry has already learned to reach and sell to new audiences. If you haven't applied games to marketing, advertising, or brand management, you'll want to get and study this book—or it could be game over for you."

—Jonathan Epstein, CEO, In-Game
Ad Firm DoubleFusion, and Founding CEO, Gamespot.com

"Crowdsourcing today has barely scratched the surface of what applied gaming mechanics can do for companies looking to complete work ranging from logos to complex software systems to automobiles in a meritocracy. Along this very same vein, individuals competing or collaborating on these bodies of work align or better define the company's brand and identity and carry the marketing message while participating. Mr. Zichermann and Ms. Linder detail how the future of marketing depends on this level of engagement and the rise of Funware in today's information space."

—Mike Martoccia, Futurist
and Crowdsourcing Expert, @mmartoccia

"My 13-year-old cousin recently said 'If I can't get an achievement for that, I'm not doing it.' Game-Based Marketing clearly shows how to leverage this emerging generation's hunger for games in every sphere of life."

—Alan Yu, ngmoco

game-based
marketing

game-based marketing

Inspire Customer Loyalty Through Rewards, Challenges, and Contests

GABE ZICHERMANN

AND

JOSELIN LINDER

WILEY

John Wiley & Sons, Inc.

Copyright © 2010 by Jargonlab, Inc. and Joselin Linder. All rights reserved.

Published by John Wiley & Sons, Inc., Hoboken, New Jersey.

Published simultaneously in Canada.

No part of this publication may be reproduced, stored in a retrieval system, or transmitted in any form or by any means, electronic, mechanical, photocopying, recording, scanning, or otherwise, except as permitted under Section 107 or 108 of the 1976 United States Copyright Act, without either the prior written permission of the Publisher, or authorization through payment of the appropriate per-copy fee to the Copyright Clearance Center, Inc., 222 Rosewood Drive, Danvers, MA 01923, (978) 750-8400, fax (978) 646-8600, or on the web at www.copyright.com. Requests to the Publisher for permission should be addressed to the Permissions Department, John Wiley & Sons, Inc., 111 River Street, Hoboken, NJ 07030, (201) 748-6011, fax (201) 748-6008, or online at http://www.wiley.com/go/permissions.

Limit of Liability/Disclaimer of Warranty: While the publisher and author have used their best efforts in preparing this book, they make no representations or warranties with respect to the accuracy or completeness of the contents of this book and specifically disclaim any implied warranties of merchantability or fitness for a particular purpose. No warranty may be created or extended by sales representatives or written sales materials. The advice and strategies contained herein may not be suitable for your situation. You should consult with a professional where appropriate. Neither the publisher nor author shall be liable for any loss of profit or any other commercial damages, including but not limited to special, incidental, consequential, or other damages.

For general information on our other products and services or for technical support, please contact our Customer Care Department within the United States at (800) 762-2974, outside the United States at (317) 572-3993 or fax (317) 572-4002.

Wiley also publishes its books in a variety of electronic formats. Some content that appears in print may not be available in electronic books. For more information about Wiley products, visit our web site atwww.wiley.com.

Library of Congress Cataloging-in-Publication Data:

Zichermann, Gabe, 1974–
    Game-based marketing: inspire customer loyalty through rewards, challenges, and contests / Gabe Zichermann & Joselin Linder.
        p. cm.
Includes bibliographical references.
ISBN: 978-0-470-56223-9 (cloth)
1. Customer loyalty programs. 2. Customer loyalty. 3. Marketing. I. Linder, Joselin, 1975– II. Title.
HF 5415.525.Z53 2010
658.8′12—dc22   2009044774

Printed in the United States of America

10 9 8 7 6 5 4 3 2 1

CONTENTS

CHAPTER 8   The Future of Gamers: Generation G   161

**CHAPTER 9   Motivating Sales with Funware: Getting
Employees into the Game   181**

CHAPTER 10   Everyone Wins: Games in Your Business   197

ACKNOWLEDGMENTS

Many thanks to all those who agreed to be interviewed for this book, on and off the record. Thanks to our agent, Molly Lyons, and everyone at Delbourgo and Associates. Also thanks to the editorial team at John Wiley & Sons, Inc., for their energy and commitment to getting this project to market. Special thanks to Dan Ambrosio, Christine Moore, and Ashley Allison.

Gabe would like to thank the following: Dean Takahashi, editor of *VentureBeat*, for his enthusiasm and evangelism for the Funware concept; his mother, father, and David for their unflinching support throughout the years; Mary and Vera for their love and affection; his sister, Sandra Zichermann, for her inspirational commitment to her intellectual pursuits; and Jason, the only one who could have handled video game, frequent flyer, and television widowerhood with as much grace, brilliance, and humor all these years.

Joselin would like to thank Wendy Bassin, Tim Deman, Marni Fechter, Karen Kaplan, Caroline Palmer, Kevin Reardon, and Sam Richie. Special thanks to Chris Tiné and San Tong. Thanks to Jim Shulman for his extensive knowledge, among other things, of the Boy Scouts. Also thanks to Jackie, Gram, Hilary, Brian, and the kids for their unending support;

to her mother, Rhoda Linder, for her unparalleled PR skills among family and friends; and her father, William Linder, for illustrating fine business savvy in his life. Finally, thank you to Aaron for being the best teamate a girl could have.

FOREWORD

W hat would Don Draper say about Funware?

In the 30 or so years that I've been in the advertising industry, I've seen just about every kind of games-meet-marketing combination. As the former chairman & CEO of Universal McCann, I helped launch media for Microsoft's Xbox and Halo Franchises, among countless other brands. Today, as CEO of NYC-based Rebel Digital, I help brilliant entrepreneurs start and scale their Internet businesses, an ever-increasing number of which are baking games into their strategy.

But the writing has been on the wall for some time.

I first got into advertising in the late 1970s in London. I joined Saatchi & Saatchi, an aggressive new wave advertising agency taking on established American giants such as McCann-Erickson, JWT, and Young & Rubicam.

Just as Don Draper rules the agency roost in the TV show *Mad Men*, so too did the creative directors at major ad agencies during this time. I was trained in media buying and later media planning. In those days, the creative teams regarded media people like me as unexciting and accounting-esque. Their motto: media is a necessary evil but best avoided at all costs!

Fortunately for all of us, media folks didn't disappear the way *Mad Men* might have you believe.

In the early 1990s, I was working at a second-generation ad agency startup called Leagas Delaney. Tim Delaney was the highly decorated genius copywriter who ruled the creative roost. In a complementary fashion, I thought of myself as a media guy with a creative eye. I hated the numbers side of my business and was always looking for opportunities to find new and engaging ways to reach consumers. Tim had a grudging respect for media, but it only went so far, as I was to shortly learn to my detriment.

We at Leagas Delaney won, against all the odds, the European advertising account for Adidas, the famous world-leading sports brand. At the time, Leagas Delaney was only operating in the United Kingdom, but our appointment was to handle a European—and eventually global—marketing campaign.

After celebrating the win, we got down to business. My first task was to find a media company that could execute our media plans across Europe. Interestingly, Carat, the one I didn't choose, happened to headhunt me shortly thereafter to head up their European centralized media management group. They didn't get our business because I wanted an agency that would be more directly responsive to Tim's creative energy. As most of my contemporaries did, I believed in the power of creative advertising to change hearts and minds.

At this point, pretty much anything Tim proposed creatively, Adidas bought. We were in the honeymoon period, and he had some radical ideas to attack Nike's dominance. Every media owner heavily courted me, right across Europe, seeking an opportunity to participate in our marquee account.

But a radical idea was brewing in our London offices. Although video games were in their infancy, I was introduced to them as an advertising platform by a couple of young Turks who were gamers themselves. The opportunities back then were limited, and it wasn't something that was on the radar of most agencies. I decided to explore the channel to see what it could offer Adidas in the way of exposure.

The gaming guys were eager to meet. We had great sessions, and it was clear that this was a huge opportunity and something that would put Adidas on the map. After all, Europe's rapidly changing youth population was spending up to 20 hours a week playing video games. These were hours they weren't watching television, and the meaning of that was not lost on me.

So, armed with data and the enthusiasm of the younger members of my team, I excitedly entered Tim's inner sanctum with two brilliant, ground-breaking, and creative video game ideas.

The first was to simply place Adidas inside a soccer game. Adidas would provide the kit with the logos, have its brand displayed on the perimeter boards that line the pitch, and run Tim's commercials on the big screen at half time. As soccer is the number one game across Europe, we felt this concept would be massive.

The second idea—totally mine—was to hire out cinemas across Europe on Saturday mornings to run video game competitions. We'd find the best player in each market and then have a tournament to find Europe's top player. There would be plenty of free media exposure, branded prizes, and the adoration of kids everywhere. Meanwhile, Adidas would "own" these venues on Saturday mornings, promoting their products directly to their target consumer. Brilliant, I thought.

I was so excited and proud of myself I could hardly get the words out. Tim listened, nodded, and seemed to be intrigued.

Then he said what he really thought.

"Get the f*@k out of my office and never, ever come back with your stupid ideas. You understand nothing about brands and creativity. Stick to numbers on a spreadsheet, and leave the creative to those who know best."

I was speechless, which is rare. To this day, I can still hear Tim's voice and remember what that moment felt like.

Of course, it was a great wake-up call for me, as I shortly left the firm for greener, more creatively welcoming pastures. While incomprehensible to me, it seems to have taken almost 20 years for the advertising industry to understand what we knew then: games are the preferred medium of youth, and therefore, they are the future.

Of course, *Game-Based Marketing* is not solely a book about advertising in games or vice versa. Just as media folks have become substantially more influential over ad agency output, so too have games transcended being an "out there" platform for conveying a brand's message. Today, basic game advertising is a must-have part of any major marketing campaign—but truly sophisticated marketers understand that its power is substantially greater.

The concept of this book—and the premise of Funware—is disarmingly simple. That every customer-company interaction can and should be made more fun is a meaningful concept in itself. But *Game-Based Marketing*'s true message is that games are power. Savvy marketers can use game mechanics to engender short-term excitement and long-term customer loyalty. This is the true power of games, and its time is now.

I think Don Draper and Tim Delaney would agree.

Robin Kent
CEO, Rebel Digital
www.rebeldigital.com
New York, NY

"The purpose of a company is to create and keep customers."

—Dr. Theodore Levitt, renowned economist
and Harvard Business School professor

INTRODUCTION

I t is September 4, 2008—the day of the opening game of the U.S. National Football League season.

Millions of Americans are sitting in their living rooms flanked by beer, friends, and food as the New York Giants kick off against the Washington Redskins. The Giants score 10 of their total 16 points in the first quarter. The Redskins score a touchdown in the second. The game is close. Tensions run high.

Cut to commercial—but not just any $3 million spot. One of the most highly anticipated marketing campaigns of the decade is about to debut. In marketing speak, these ads appear to have the four P's in spades—Price, Place, Product, and especially Promotion. In fact, if these spots are packing as much heat as they promise, they have added a fifth P to that list: Power. After all, it is the rapt attention of a nation that makes advertisers spend over $20 billion a year on NFL advertising.

That very day, the world's most successful technology company, Microsoft—under the guidance of marketing powerhouse Crispin Porter + Bogusky—would unveil a $300 million ad campaign featuring one of the most recognizable and lauded celebrities of our day: Jerry Seinfeld. With genius and philanthropist Bill Gates on board, word of the campaign achieved mythological proportions faster than its competition could croak, "I'm a Mac." In the massive lead up to the launch, pundits in the mainstream media held an almost sycophantic belief in the inevitable success of this series of commercials. After all, how could such a combination be anything but successful?

When the first of Microsoft's three spots premiered that September day, its audience bore witness to Seinfeld and

3

Gates as they squared off in a suburban shopping mall, one-liners tossed around like a pigskin at a tailgate party. Ninety seconds later, fade to black.

Metaphorically appropriate in the scheme of things, the Giants only scored one more touchdown that game, missing the extra point. Meanwhile, the Redskins took their nine-point loss and went home. When the dust settled, another, even more important score was tallied. Social networking: 1. Advertising: 0.

The commercial unleashed a massive social-networking supported backlash. With two more ads awaiting release, Microsoft pulled the plug on the whole campaign despite having already released the second spot into the wild. Worse still, social networks turned the videos viral in an exceedingly negative way. Anyone with a Facebook, Twitter, or MySpace account knew about Microsoft's advertising disaster; and they were looking, analyzing, and laughing out loud.

The now infamous commercial went like this: Microsoft chairman and cofounder Bill Gates tries on shoes at a discount shoe store. Funnyman Jerry Seinfeld coaches him along the way. Peppered with a series of irrelevant and insipid observations by Seinfeld, the scene shows Gates, appearing in turn either bewildered or speechless (not unlike the viewing audience), bumbling through the aimless plot. Finally, the tag line "The Future, Delicious" appears and—gratefully—ends the spot.

Although he was indicted, Jerry Seinfeld didn't kill advertising. In fact, only a few years earlier, he had achieved great success hawking American Express cards. It took hundreds of people, a lot of money, and more than one grievous humiliation to mark the beginning of the end for the modern ad campaign.

Unfortunately for Microsoft and its partners, where once a failed commercial could just lie down quietly and die with a few in-the-know tradesmen sniggering behind the scenes, suddenly there was an audience to those failures. Through the Seinfeld-Microsoft campaign failure, it suddenly became clear that in a socially networked world, the quiet ridicule had given way to blaring mockery and a pointing of fingers, piling shame upon the campaign and its makers.

Damage control was called in. Microsoft insisted it had never intended on using Seinfeld in more than two spots anyway. Further, company representatives claimed that while they would have preferred a favorable audience response to the commercial, the reaction "was not unexpected."

But multihundred-million-dollar ad campaigns do not just materialize. There were probably more person-hours spent working on the Seinfeld-Microsoft spot than people in the stadium for the NFL opening game itself. Beyond concept and creative approval, there are extensive test screenings and revisions. So, if the problem isn't that marketers lack research discipline, funding, or creative talent, why do so many advertising campaigns fail? Why has advertising become a hit-driven business in itself, like movies or TV? More important, does it have to be?

From Coca-Cola's jolly Santa to Wendy's "Where's the Beef?" lady, advertising has been at times both iconic and culturally transformative. But the cost-benefit is difficult to anticipate, and even worse, its failures now stand on the public stage of social networking. Further, competition is plentiful and loud and includes TiVo, mute buttons, and the general din of a business world competing for the waning attention of consumers who are far more interested in *Guitar Hero*, *World of Warcraft*, and *American Idol*.

This brings us to the final culprit, the last piercing arrow into the heart of the Taco Bell Chihuahua: games. People are not only playing them; they are watching others play them.

They are increasingly replacing every form of entertainment with games themselves. In other words, fun is the latest competitor for consumer attention.

Why should people stop having fun to watch a commercial? More important, why would they? Fundamentally, how do marketers get anyone's attention anymore, much less that of Generation G, the greatest game-playing demographic in history? The answer is simple and unequivocal: in order to compete with games, marketing must become a game.

In this socially networked, choice-driven world, the old methods of reaching consumers with advertising messages have simply stopped working as well as they need to. Game mechanics, on the other hand, are steadily rising to the surface. In everything from the airline you fly to the ATM card you use, savvy marketers are turning to the power of games to increase their return on investment, provide essential predictability, and—above all else—engender the kind of customer loyalty that wasn't before possible.

Whereas marketers have used "traditional" loyalty programs and advergames for years to create engagement and buzz, this book—and the movement it represents—is focused on integrating the power of games into every aspect of product marketing and promotions. Understanding this opportunity will empower you to create breakthrough strategies that leverage the power of social networks and human behavior in ways designed to cut your marketing costs and bolster your bottom line. Whether you're a small start-up or top global brand, *Game-Based Marketing* offers important lessons—both positive and negative—from the greatest game-marketing innovators of the day. In short, *Game-Based Marketing* is a primer for leveraging the unprecedented opportunity created by the game-centric revolution in marketing and advertising.

In many ways, Jerry Seinfeld's work on the Microsoft campaign heralded the beginning of this new era. Like a mashup of Paul Revere and the court jester, Seinfeld has shown us that both "the Gamers are coming" and the emperor has no clothes. As with the tectonic shifts in comedy unveiled by his groundbreaking show in the 1990s, a fundamental change is afoot, and the force behind it is virtually unstoppable.

The future of marketing is games, and it starts today.

Visit funwareblog.com to see the Seinfeld-Gates commercials and discuss when you think advertising finally "jumped the shark."

 Summary

- Marketers don't lack research discipline, funding, or creative talent, yet many advertising campaigns fail.
- Advertising has become a hit-driven business in itself, like movies or television.
- The cost-benefit of brand advertising is difficult to anticipate.
- Failures are much more public due to social networking and the Internet.
- Ads are now competing with games.
- Games represent unprecedented opportunities in marketing.

The Argument for Loyalty

S ince its founding in 1926, NBC News has amassed one of the world's most important—and valuable—video archives. And although the company had previously used its historical video content for its own editorial purposes and sold access to major educational institutions, key executives at the $17 billion-plus NBC/Universal media conglomerate felt that a major business opportunity was being missed. After all, this content—from moon landings to assassinations—had to be worth more than the minor revenues it was generating per year, or else perhaps it had become truly priceless. But despite the positive cachet of using such a term, pricelessness is a bad thing when running a for-profit entity.

Put another, understated way, "We had a business challenge," said Chris Tiné, veteran TV producer and one of the driving forces behind what would become a thoroughly innovative and ground-breaking movement in traditional media: the *gamification* of news.

Tiné continued, "We're sitting on this archive of amazing video clips of NBC News. How do we get these clips in front of an audience so they can have meaningful interactions?"

For Tiné, the goal was twofold: one, to get this valuable footage of American and worldwide history out from archival purgatory, and two, to create a new profit center for the company. In both cases, NBC succeeded through *games*.

With the creation of iCue, an educational software application used in high schools as a supplemental studying tool for Advanced Placement classes, Tiné managed to create a system whereby NBC's extensive footage was put to good use.

"Video trivia was not the first idea we had," he explained, "but the more we started to brainstorm, think, and roll ideas around, the more we loved the idea of building a game that would engage students, teachers, and parents." While iCue continues to receive extensive plaudits as a breakthrough initiative in engaging learning communities with history, it was the next step in NBC's video evolution that truly set the company apart.

In 2008, the group launched *What's Your IQ?* a game built for Facebook, one of the fastest-growing social networking sites, as a side project to iCue. *What's Your IQ?* is a video trivia game that leverages hundreds of hours of NBC News film and video footage, wraps trivia around it, and allows users to play against their friends, join teams, earn badges, and climb levels—all within the Facebook platform. Of course, this was a substantial challenge, especially considering that YouTube is a completely free video service with billions of hours of content available at the ready—and no educational "wrapper" to discourage casual players seeking distraction instead of learning.

Against that backdrop, Tiné and his team focused on using Facebook to drive traffic to the iCue site. Then something unexpected happened: *What's Your IQ?* itself began generating substantial viral usage and, unbelievably, revenue.

The process turned out to be simpler than anyone could have imagined. By making a fun game, "[advertiser] brands realized they got to associate themselves with outstanding video content," said Tiné, "not to mention, a sticky application."

By "sticky," Tiné meant that *What's Your IQ?* routinely attracted well over 100,000 users per month (the peak usage of NBC News online is 2.4 million streams viewed per week). But more importantly, most of these users were dedicating meaningful hours playing the game. And why? The game's design itself was focused on fun first and business (or educational) objectives second. In the process of designing their product this way, the iCue team discovered something very important: they could create a sticky user experience that generates positive brand value and cash while building long-term loyalty.

While most advertisers today find themselves struggling to achieve even one of these objectives clearly, the iCue team—and countless others—have learned that only games can cut through the clutter of a crowded brand marketplace and socially networked environment to attract, retain, and monetize consumers like no other.

"Stickiness" Is Loyalty

The idea of "sticky content" isn't new, although the term has mostly been associated with Web sites. The basic concept is that stickiness is a qualitative measure, most closely aligned with two standard Internet metrics: time spent on a site and number of repeat visits per user. When you consider those statistics together, you get a composite view of a site's stickiness.

When applied outside the world of the Web, stickiness is often referred to by another name: loyalty. When a coffee buyer chooses Starbucks over Pete's Coffee every day or a TV viewer continues to watch David Letterman over Conan O'Brien at 11:30 p.m., we call that loyalty. The same motivators and paradigms apply regardless of whether we are looking at offline or online worlds.

While the vagaries of the economy or radical shifts in the competitive marketplace can profoundly affect the expression of loyalty, it is nonetheless the most enduring bond between a product, brand, or company and its customers. As products become commoditized, it is loyalty—pure and simple—that keeps people buying. Loyalty is consumers' expression of brand preference and their repayment of the equity you've invested in the relationship.

On the Web, the stickiest sites are social networking and multiplayer games. As illustrated in subsequent chapters, they have more in common than meets the eye at first. In the offline world, the most successful loyalty programs are those run by airlines and other hospitality companies. Online, hundreds of millions of game-players spend billions of minutes each month chasing points, levels, badges, and rewards—both real and psychological. At the airport and in the supermarket, similar numbers make choices every day, with their real time and money, placing these virtual currencies ahead of their real-world counterparts.

What if we could combine the best of both online and offline programs by taking the superior elements of each and weaving them into a fun and long-term customer loyalty program?

We can. And *Game-Based Marketing* is the guide to this brave new world of customer engagement through Funware: the application of game mechanics to everyday situations. Many innovative companies and organizations already understand the power of games and are well on their way to reshaping industries from financial services to space exploration. Undoubtedly, the rise of generations weaned on games and the promise of Funware will reshape your industry, too.

Playing with Loyalty

Look in anyone's mail, wallet, or inbox and you are certain to notice a common thread: loyalty programs are everywhere, and like it or not, we are all invested in them. If you are like 80 percent of Americans, you probably have one or two credit cards that are earning points and seven or more frequent traveler accounts that are open, of which three to four are active across airlines, hotels, and car rental agencies. You may even be among the top echelon of "casual" rewards program players, having responded to a promotion or eaten at a particular restaurant in order to earn bonus points sometime in the last year. And if you're like most of us, you have tales of great success (like landing a luxury oceanfront suite in Tahiti for your honeymoon) and outrageous failure (perhaps having to pay $250 in taxes and fees for that free ticket) to recount about your journey through the loyalty program universe.

Does it ever feel like you're playing a game with your preferred airline for those free First Class tickets, one where you can't stop collecting points even though you can't always redeem them for the rewards you want? Whether you know it or not, *you are*.

But what *is* a loyalty program if not a complex, multilayered, gamelike exercise in achieving status, rewards, and special treatment? Whether you seek free upgrades, a Gold Card, or entrance into the Red Carpet lounge while waiting at the airport, what you are invariably seeking is a *win*. The underlying drive to keep playing based on a belief that you will someday win those rewards is exactly the type of motivation that gives loyalty programs their power.

Of course, for those who know the game is afoot, the entire frequent flyer program (FFP) experience is radically different than for those who don't. Millions of players are at this moment counting, calculating, and strategizing their next loyalty moves as readily as if they were playing *World of Warcraft*, *Bridge*, or *Klondike Solitaire*. As loyalty programs bump up against the social Web, countless sites and discussion forums have been launched in order to help players play better and win more. This of course has fed a cycle of increasing complexity in the loyalty program world, thereby creating a marketing opportunity for brands that promise to simplify the process. Capital One's "No Hassle Rewards" card program is one example; it allows consumers to earn points on their credit cards and offers cash back and airline miles, among other rewards that suit their lifestyles.

The Future of Loyalty—Frequent Flyer Games

Unlike most generic loyalty systems, such as those found at grocery stores or gas stations, FFPs have gone far beyond their humble roots as mildly sophisticated versions of rebate schemes. Today's FFPs make use of a number of key design features torn straight from a hardcore videogame designer's playbook, including points, levels, badges, challenges, and rewards, to create the most sophisticated form of loyalty that exists between brand and customer.

Traditional Rebate Program	Frequent Flyer Program
Perceived value must be attached directly to rewards (e.g. "buy 10 cups of coffee, get one free")	Perceived value is attached indirectly to rewards
Purchases are rewarded with credits that may be converted into rewards	Purchases as well as other behaviors and the successful completion of challenges are rewarded with credits that may be converted into rewards
The more points you earn, the larger the reward (at direct cost to the business)	The more points earned, the more opportunities to advance in status and level, as well as a wide range of possible rewards of varying costs
Points and rewards are the only gamelike features	Challenges, opportunities for team play, and complex game design encourage players to continue playing
Other than points and rewards, players are rarely offered a	Airports establish real-world opportunities for players to

Traditional Rebate Program	Frequent Flyer Program
"world" in which their play is recognized and valued	"show off" status and move forward at little cost (once established) to the airlines
Could benefit from a more complex virtual game in which points are empowered through virtual rewards	Could benefit from a more complex virtual game in which points are empowered through virtual rewards

Put another way, while only some consumers have become aware of the game dynamic at play, FFP designers—travel brand marketers—have become thoroughly sentient, launching an increasing number of campaigns that mirror game challenges almost exactly. For example, the United Airlines' Team Frequent Flyer Challenge of 2008 encouraged customers to register teams in order to track points together over the better part of a year. The offer was a simple promise of status and 50 million frequent flyer points to be distributed among each team's players.

FFPs are particularly and extraordinarily powerful. They routinely cause players engaged in the game to make decisions that are counterintuitive to their well-being—and checkbook—in order to "level up." For example, flyers will choose inconvenient or more expensive flights simply to earn points or levels with a particular carrier, even when the direct option was cheaper or more convenient. Some players even opt to take flights entirely for the purpose of earning points or miles in the run up to the end of the year (known as a *mileage run*).

Thus, one of the most unheralded achievements of the FFP is how thoroughly its designers have altered behavior in *real life*—not in a parallel virtual world but here and now, with real cash and time. In fact, if frequent flyers *didn't* make these counterintuitive choices—and there wasn't some arbitrage on rewards available—airlines wouldn't continue offering FFPs.

Even low-cost airlines such as Southwest, JetBlue, and Virgin America have implemented loyalty programs; it seems almost impossible to imagine launching a meaningful travel brand—of any stripe—without one. Therefore, while the raw success of FFPs is self-evident—and their entrenched nature in our culture unmistakable, the real story is often told by the game's most hardcore players. And in the case of frequent flyers, it is told on a site called Flyertalk.com.

Communities of Influence: Flyertalk

Launched in the mid-1990s, Flyertalk is currently the world's most popular destination for reward program players. The site boasts over 500,000 unique visitors per month and nearly 12 million posted discussion items covering hotels, airlines, cars, credit cards, and every alternative method for obtaining points, rewards, and status. The site's influence is so substantial in the hospitality industry that most major brands have full-time ambassadors to Flyertalk. Some companies, like travel search engine ITA, even have beta products built and maintained solely for the community.

But it isn't just the raw number of Flyertalkers that makes them so interesting to travel and tourism brands; it's their *engagement* and *influence* that sets them apart from the market. They are, in effect, the top-ranked players, earning and spending billions of the games' currency (points). They also profoundly influence others and affect the design of the game itself.

It's here on Flyertalk, with its devotion to the oft-maligned FFP that we discover that the game designer has real power over the real lives of real people. And no advertisement has ever come close in its ability to get consumers to act against their own self-interest with as much predictability as the FFP design.

Of course, with the power of *any* game design comes great responsibility, whether they're being used to enthrall teens in a virtual world for 50 hours a week or to divert 50-something businesspeople halfway around the world to gain some points and free lounge access. While the two aforementioned players are profoundly different individuals with markedly distinct needs and motivations, they are both inescapably *players*. And as we'll clearly demonstrate, they like to *win*.

So what does the omnipresent FFP have to do with marketing, and how does it differ from a stock-in-trade loyalty program? The answer lies in the exploitation of fundamental human desire through game design for a business purpose. This design philosophy borrows heavily from games but remains firmly rooted in the science of persuasion, and it is called Funware.

Funware: Putting Fun into Everything

Funware—a term that summarizes the ubiquitous presence of games or game mechanics in our lives—also serves as the buzzword for game-based marketing. By becoming more aware of the Funware in which we are already engaging, either as a marketer or as a consumer, we are increasing our ability to produce a desired outcome. In other words, if one remains a passive participant in these games—either as a brand or player—encouraging specific behaviors that lead to desired outcomes is more difficult. The core premise of Funware for marketers is its ability to drive user behavior in a predictable, overt, and focused way. Put another way: Funware is the art and science of turning your customers' everyday interactions into "games" that serve your business purposes.

As Funware gains momentum and more resources and money are earmarked for its development, we will watch as an inevitable transformation takes shape: the leveraging of the power of games and the emergence of a game-centric culture to create tremendous value. Its practitioners will also gain untold advantage over their rivals. In short, the future of Funware and game design in business is breathtaking. In the meantime, however, the world is full of mistakes and missed opportunities that game design can leverage for the best possible end.

Chase "Goes Dutch"

A good example of Funware done partially right is JPMorgan Chase & Co.'s 2009 program called *Chase Picks Up the Tab*. The simple premise: the bank will randomly reimburse a particular charge, using slot machine game mechanics, when a customer uses his or her Chase credit or debit card to make point-of-sale purchases. Simple, catchy, and clever, the campaign revives an earlier version that was well regarded by consumers.

But Chase has missed two great opportunities with the campaign's design. First, in order to get into the game, you must have a Chase account. It's extremely difficult for non-Chase customers to become involved because they aren't provided an easy method by which to sign up for and play the game, leaving out a majority of prospective players and restricting the game's potential bottom-line impact. It is unlikely that Chase simply intends that existing customers use their debit cards more often; that's a fairly low-yield objective. The company is more likely hoping that *Chase Picks Up the Tab* will bring in new accounts. Unfortunately, the game makes the barriers to entry for noncustomers extremely high, putting it decidedly out of their reach. The end result is that the company may find itself less likely to meet its intended goals.

The game could easily be improved by adding a virtual (or literal) scratch card for nonaccount holders. For example, by signing up your mobile phone number, Chase might periodically text you an offer to buy something at a certain moment from a particular merchant with a chance for reimbursement or maybe they would allow you to redeem a cash rebate for simply entering any Chase branch in real time. Frankly, the company could even leverage an online service to literally offer rebates to users of other banks' cards. Any of these options would generate a substantially greater impact, leveraging the free-to-play theory of game-based business models.

Second, like most contests or sweepstakes, the Chase program is limited in its loyalty effect. Once the promotion ends, the relative increase in usage does, too. By extending the campaign's impact across years instead of weeks, the gameplay wouldn't have to end—and neither would the customer's interest in playing.

The Free-to-Play Design

"Free-to-play" has become a mantra of successful online game design in recent years. Originating in high-piracy countries like China and Korea, the concept is to offer game experiences entirely for free (and with easy registration) in perpetuity. Then, premium game features and

(continued)

(*continued*)

customizations are offered in exchange for cash or in-game points. Revenue is typically earned by bringing large numbers of people into the funnel (the notion of free helps immensely with this) and then encouraging 2 percent to 10 percent of players to buy these upgrades. With sufficient scale and over time, free-to-play game developers are generating more revenue and engagement with consumers than traditional $50 per unit approaches.

Extended to Funware, the free-to-play philosophy posits that users should be offered the easiest possible path into your "game." Strip down the barriers to signing up as much as possible, and focus your energy on getting users to increase their engagement over the long term by investing small amounts of cash, time, and social capital. This innovative design philosophy is sure to yield improved long-term results and more closely reflect the expectations of the next generation of players.

Another way Chase might curry business is by offering prizes in real time at its automated banking machines. One of the simplest ideas would be to give out random cash rewards coincident with a withdrawal. Non-Chase customers might be more likely to pay fees if a chance to win $100 is on the table. Similarly, existing customers could be encouraged to use the nearest Chase ATM thereby maximizing fee potential.

As it stands, *Chase Picks Up the Tab* misses great opportunities to create deep, abiding loyalty for existing consumers and to generate interest in Chase's product among nonmembers. Whether this matters is dependent on the bank's objective; if simply maintaining customers and encouraging Chase card and ATM use are the goals, *Chase Picks Up the Tab* has been a roaring success. But if new user growth is an objective, the campaign is half-baked.

Undoubtedly, part of whatever success this promotion *has* enjoyed lies in the fact that money is the reward for playing. And many marketers continue to believe that the best (sometimes, *only*) prize that truly motivates consumers is cash. But is this true? Again, multiplayer games offer a clear answer.

The Value of Prizes

People have always been obsessed with winning.

And somewhat bizarrely, people have also always been obsessed with watching *other* people win—or lose. Examples are limitless and range from sports (evidence of which can be found in the earliest of ancient cultures) to politics. It is therefore unsurprising that the game show began very early in the architecture of TV's history. In fact, on July 1, 1941—the first officially recognized day of television broadcasting—the long-running game show *Truth or Consequences* was among the very first programs unveiled.

While spectator sports were nothing new, consider this: the success of the TV game show relied on an audience sitting at home and watching a stranger play a game, one that lacked any physical action—no running, hitting, or movement of almost any kind. People simply stood still and answered questions, solved puzzles, or pushed a buzzer. By and large, audience members did not get to participate. They themselves could never win and rarely had any familial or geographic connection to the players. And yet they continued to watch.

People are inherently drawn to tense situations, and an intrinsic aspect of games is that they bring tension to the table. The popularity of the TV game show reflects a basic truth about play and winning in our society: even people who aren't overly competitive like to win, even if they define success differently.

In the world of marketing games, loyalty programs do not always require a monetary or "valuable" reward in order for a player to take an interest in a game's outcome. Simply put, much of the value a player gets from the game itself is psychological. For example, frequent flyer miles do not convert to cash very easily, yet the promise of a future reward ("someday I'll go to Tahiti") and the idea of getting something for nothing are enough to motivate the most casual players.

Historical Funware

Three Successful Low-Cost Prizes

- **Cracker Jack® Rubber Face (1931):** A 1 1/4 × 1 3/4 inch piece of rubber with a face printed on it. By pushing on the back of the object with a finger, the winner of this prize could distort the face at will.

- **Kellogg's® X-Ray Viewer (1989):** This fabulous piece of technological genius incorporated a tiny peephole through a cardboard frame said to give anyone who looked through it x-ray vision. A piece of film etched with an image of a bone did most of the work, but still, you knew you wanted it.

- **McDonald's® Grimace Eraser Happy Meal Toy (1979):** Better than the Ronald McDonald plastic hand puppets employees passed out with the original Happy Meals when the intended prizes had run out, these purple erasers got many a kid out of a tight spot as they attempted to follow the mazes on the Happy Meal boxes.

A crucial point is that by reevaluating what constitutes a reward, marketers may be surprised to note that what prompts people to enter a sweepstakes is rarely the promise of that shiny new car but rather the overarching enthusiasm for the experience of playing the game itself. Status, success, and even sociability are key drivers of gamelike behavior in individuals.

Even more exciting is the prospect that games do not always require a competitive element in order to make them notable. In fact, many of the most successful and enduring game designs are either self-reflective, like solitaire or cooperative, like a scavenger hunt.

Simply put, game mechanics and the psychological conditions they exploit are powerful tools that marketers can use, and they're a lot cheaper—and more effective—than cash in the long run.

Game Mechanics

A game mechanic is any technique implemented by game designers in order to create play. For example, a *leaderboard*, a ranked list of players, can be used as a game mechanic if it is intended to generate activity. A game mechanic also applies to individual parts of the games themselves. Many Web sites have used short puzzle challenges, for example as indirect elements to encourage play in a larger game, or *metagame*.

One recognizable example of a game mechanic is the scratch card element of McDonald's annual *Monopoly* game. The scratch card is a minigame (and potential instant win) that the consumer plays as part of a larger $1 million prize sweepstakes. In order to play the larger game, the consumer must begin with this scratch card. This minigame is designed to encourage repeat play and ultimately, repeat visits to McDonald's in order to win. While simplistic, adding these minigames raises the overall fun level (and thus, engagement) of the endeavor as a whole.

There are few life experiences, *including* games, that couldn't be made more fun through the application of even more sophisticated game mechanics and designs. This is a fact to which most game designers freely admit, and something even McDonald's could learn from. Adding game mechanics doesn't always mean complicating the experience. It is enough for some people to simply buy lunch and receive a game card in order to take an interest in building a Monopoly.

But why stop there? What if McDonald's included an alternative reality game with its *Monopoly* game? For example, a player could register online in a particular city and instead of collecting pieces to complete the board, he or she could virtually "collect" McDonald's locations by visiting them and buying something in real life. Examples might include a Baron-of-Boston challenge (visit every McDonald's location in greater Boston) or a Two-on-Tuesday challenge (buy something at two different stores on a Tuesday.

This simple, quick suggestion could open the door to a vastly more sophisticated, engaging, and far-reaching version of McDonald's *Monopoly*. As described, the game and challenges could feature single-player and group options and be infinitely replayable. Moreover, the game could be played over the span of years instead of just during the weeks of the promotion. In this way, the application of Funware can benefit even long-established and highly successful campaigns as easily as it can move the needle for less sophisticated companies.

The Future of Funware

Few businesses couldn't benefit by adding Funware components to their marketing plan. Throughout the book, we will highlight Funware marketing ideas for established businesses in order to illustrate the potential for prodigious and effective game development.

Barnes & Noble Funware

Objective: Increase regular customers' repeat visits to Barnes & Noble and encourage customers who are intimidated by the concentration of book stacks to buy more comfortably.

Game mechanic: Create a leaderboard for the top 10 book genres in the store and list the individuals who lead in book purchases within each genre.

Outcome: Customers buying the most books in the biography, fiction, crime, and poetry sections would be rewarded by Barnes & Noble simply by treating their purchases as accomplishments. Thus, by purchasing and reading more books, users would climb the ladder toward "expert" status at B & N.

Win condition: The board leaders for each genre would be awarded a badge indicating their status as a store expert on their respective topic, alerting fellow customers that they can be asked for recommendations (either online or in person). Experts might even be able to schedule "master classes" with interested customers and post their bios on the store's Web site so that neophytes could book appointments to meet with them.

(*continued*)

(*continued*)

Note: As with all games, there is the potential for exploitation in this simple design. For example, players could "game the system" simply by purchasing more books than others, creating the opportunity for nonexpert winners. A solution might be to allow users to peer review each other with simple quizzes or commentary about books they have read, thereby establishing trust in the experts.

Don't Hate the Player, Hate the Game

As game-play becomes increasingly enmeshed in our lives, savvy marketers have an opportunity to leverage game mechanics and Funware to create more engagement and loyalty than ever before. Adding frequent flyer–style mechanics and simplifying the process of getting consumers into a brand's gamelike experience, are simple ways to make every customer interaction more fun—and therefore more meaningful. People inherently love to play. Historically, we have delineated our lives between work and play—that is, "have to" and "want to." But the gap is closing, driven by social media and games. Interestingly, most games are played just beneath our consciousness. But that doesn't mean we're not playing. We may be passive, but our intent to win is real. And if marketers can understand and direct this instinct for passive play to their own ends, everyone will benefit.

Key Concepts:

- We are surrounded by and consistently play games.
- Frequent flyer games are among the most powerful and ubiquitous.

- Funware is a design philosophy that helps us mesh games with marketing.
- Everything can be made more fun.
- Game mechanics are levers used to drive user behavior.
- Games can be tailored to meet specific business objectives.

C H A P T E R

2

Passive Play

The Incidental Games We Play

Games have the power to irrevocably change the world. By now, you've probably heard of *World of Warcraft*, a popular online multiplayer game with more than 11.5 million active players. *World of Warcraft* is so engaging that a support group even exists for the game's "widows." In fact, there are multiple Web sites devoted to the partners of so-called *World of Warcraft* addicts, including Gamerwidow.com, where men and women come together to discuss how to entice their partners back into the real world. A brief perusal of Yahoo's *World of Warcraft* widow support group is a reminder that time dedicated to game-play can lead to unpaid bills, unbathed children, and unwalked dogs.

Still question the power of games? According to Nielsen, the average Wii, Xbox, or Playstation player spends about 12 hours per month glued to his or her TV monitor. With sweaty fingers on controllers, these players anxiously shoot, swing, and solve their way out of the challenges that game developers present. This already astonishing figure has actually risen year after year, with a 21 percent increase in 2008–2009 alone. And, shockingly, it does *not* include the dozens of hours spent playing online, PC, and mobile games favored by hundreds of millions of people worldwide.

There's even a word used by gamers and the media to describe someone with this kind of play habit: *"hard-core."* Over the past 15 years, even its pejorative meaning (the porn connotations are not incidental) has softened, and the term is regularly used to describe entire genres of games, players, and experiences. In fact, most household-name games are hard-core *by design*.

But, while the majority of people would never use the word hard-core to describe their own play habits, a quick look at the world around us confirms something we all know, refer to, and engage in without even the slightest conscious awareness: Almost everything seems to offer us an opportunity to play. Put another way, all the world's a game, and savvy marketers can—and do—leverage this fact to create lasting engagement and positive brand connections with consumers. By tapping into our innate desire to play and by harnessing the game mechanics we're already familiar with, marketers can create cost-effective loyalty that is but a point, badge, or level away.

Latte Leaders: Status and Levels

Consider your local Starbucks. The next time you're there, take note of the "Customer Service Game" as it unfolds. Upon entry, people take their places in line—young and old, tired and wired alike. They order, pay, and wait for their drink. *Order, pay, and wait*. The behaviors typically are so repetitive that one can't help but notice when they are interrupted. For example, we wonder who the person is who orders, pays, and is handed a drink without waiting. The rest of us enter the line normally and pay in sequence, but this customer's drink is ready and waiting when he arrives at the barista. Even more intriguing is the person who is handed a drink at the cash register. In game terminology, this customer has effectively "leveled up." (If he were playing *Pac-Man*, he might be snacking on bananas rather than cherries.) His stakes are higher, and his game-play is functioning at a deeper level.

In other words, he's figured something out that may not be obvious to everyone else—and as a result, he's *winning*.

What game is he playing, and how did he start to win?

It's clear that this customer has built up a rapport with the staff over time. Perhaps he orders the same drink at the same time every day. Maybe he engaged staff members in a memorable conversation about his lactose intolerance, so that when they realized he was a 9 AM regular, they easily remembered his soy milk latte. The bottom line is that the staff behind the counter came to feel confident about anticipating his drink order. Now his mornings (and afternoons) go a little faster, and the queue runs a little quicker (making the baristas happy). Everyone's a winner . . . except the poor sods who don't even know (or care) that the game is afoot.

Other levels at Starbucks include "rewards" like free flavor shots, an occasionally upsized drink, free or reduced-priced day-old muffins, or extra beverages on the house. While there are many different levels inside the game, the biggest one continues to be the ordering queue. Even more important than saving the queue-beating coffee drinker a few minutes in the morning is the status that comes from the extra power that can embolden the player—and others watching him play.

Surprisingly, few people are aware of the game inherent in this phenomenon. Most people have seen it but don't make the connection between game-play and their fellow customer's accomplishment. However, this lack of awareness should be compelling to any marketer in any business in which a lineup forms. Armed with this powerful cutting-edge knowledge, marketing teams can make this game into a win for *them*. Remember, in the case of Starbucks customers, even though a game has never been explicitly laid out for them, they have nonetheless organized themselves—willingly or otherwise—into a gamelike structure.

Black Cards and Red Carpets

After 20 years, Starbucks has begun to acknowledge its most frequent and loyal customers. By increasing the status and visibility of its most loyal group of patrons through their Black Card offering, Starbucks has come close to evolving a frequent flyer mentality. However, the company still hasn't developed a clear vision for the *red carpet* opportunity at their feet.

Where airlines have understood the value of the red carpet and priority boarding for years, Starbucks and other coffee houses have only recently discovered the power of the expedited coffee order. Consumers playing at a lower level subsequently become interested in how they might achieve this preferred treatment. Wondering what they have to do to get there opens a dialogue in which a marketer might suggest, "All you have to do is buy 10 consecutive cups of coffee."

From an operations standpoint, a business's *win* is even greater: the marginal cost of providing the red carpet experience is almost nothing. In fact, if the program is designed exactly like those offered by the airlines (pulling from both priority and standard queues, where priority goes first), businesses won't even suffer reduced aggregate throughput. Over time, more and more players will actively seek the red carpet treatment while voluntarily opting in to your marketing programs and sharing personal information with you—all for the equivalent of a slightly faster cup of coffee and the recognition that goes along with it.

Starbucks—Beyond the Menu: Tips for Leveling Up According to Baristas

- Order drinks that aren't on the main menu. These drinks are common in the Starbucks vernacular; in other words, people-in-the-know know them, but they will set you apart. Drinks include a short coffee (served in a kid's small hot chocolate cup), a Starbucks Misto (just like a café au lait but consisting of three-quarters coffee and one-quarter milk), or a Doppio on Ice (two shots of espresso to which you can add your own milk).

- Don't just leave a tip: make it obvious. If you want it to be noticed, make sure the cashier sees your money go in the tip jar.

- Be friendly: smile, make conversation, and get involved. Even if it's early, try to be polite and friendly.

(continued)

> (*continued*)
>
> - Arrive at the same time every day, and keep your order the same. Consistency will make the baristas comfortable that anticipating your order won't result in wasted coffee.

Keeping Score

Putting on a jersey, donning a pair of Air Jordans, and walking out with a team onto a basketball court is an obvious form of *active game-play*. Sitting down at the table with seven letter tiles and a board for a round of Scrabble against your grandmother is another example. However, for most consumers in the Starbucks game example, the game afoot is *passive*. That is, customers are blissfully unaware that a game is being played.

One of the leading indicators that some kind of game is being played is the presence of a scorekeeping mechanism. Typically, this takes the form of points assigned for specific activities, but it can be much broader. Scores are assigned throughout the world any time a count is kept. Sales team performance shown on a chart by the office door, comparative rankings of top honor-roll students, even the number of followers on Twitter or friends on Facebook are all forms of scorekeeping.

Understanding that people like to keep score and providing easy ways for them to do so are effortless methods by which marketers can create value and lasting loyalty. After all, would you really want to change venues once you have entered the *"high-score"* list at a café or bookstore? Similarly, being ranked just below one of your friends on a social leaderboard may motivate you to work harder, creating an opening for brands to associate themselves with goal-setting and personal accomplishment.

The Subway Scrum: Rules of Play

Savvy marketers can prosper by understanding that games are constantly taking place all around us. By looking at gaming constructs that literally erupt out of daily, even chorelike, activities, ideas for encouraging *active* game-play are even easier to spot. Taking what works in those passive games and surfacing them can help you design broadly appealing Funware for consumers.

Take the daily commute. What happens when a crowded subway pulls into a similarly crowded station? The next time you find yourself on the platform, don't take the first train that comes along. Instead, step back and observe the people getting on and off the train in real time. White lines similar to those strategizing a football game could probably be drawn. People waiting to board stand aside as the train stops but stay close enough so that their "competition" doesn't slip in ahead. Using body language to block and hold their position, they push onto the car and head for any remaining empty seat as soon as they see an opening in the flow of exiting passengers. The seat (or a better standing spot) is the primary objective, but it must be obtained within a constraint: players must not break any major rules by aggressively bumping into each other, for example. In order to win, you must use physicality without getting physical or else risk a verbal (or physical) rebuke.

In this form of passive competition, rules and game mechanics abound, yet there are no indicators of overt competition. No one calls it "The Subway Game." No one trains to get on the train—at least not directly—and no one is rewarded by the mayor of New York for having slick and well-honed skills.

However, passengers are rewarded in other ways. By not having to stand during the trip from midtown to Coney Island, they have won the (mini)game. But people waiting in line for the subway are unlikely to acknowledge that they are competing unless asked point blank, "Are you going to fight to get a seat on the subway?" The probable reply is likely, "Hell, yeah! I'm first, and if that woman tries to cut me off, I'll bodycheck her!"

We can similarly surface the underlying competitive behavior (and tension) inherent in the subway game and leverage it to create enduring loyalty. Consider Ticketmaster and American Express's longstanding partnership to offer Amex cardholders advance access to tickets for popular shows. It is not unusual for events to sell out in the first minutes after tickets go on sale, so this benefit—allowing cardholders to make purchases well before the general public—can be substantial. It's a "get-on-first "card. Although official numbers are not publicly available, anecdotal evidence suggests that a fairly sizeable number of Amex cardholders have an account largely for access to shows and events.

Regardless, the notion of scarcity of tickets for an event is an artificial construct. That is, marketers are free to decide—at their own whim—who gets the coveted item. So, you can create artificial pressure and scarcity by offering a better or limited version of your product to more loyal customers, using that as a lure to bring others into the loyalty program. There is no net effect on the revenue associated with the sale of the item specifically, but it has a substantial effect on the loyalty program itself—and, therefore, long-term revenue.

The "premium" seats offered by most airlines exemplifies the phenomenon of false scarcity. While many carriers, such

as United Airlines or British Airways, offer premium economy with distinguishing features (such as more legroom or a
segregated cabin), most airlines have begun charging for mar-
ginally better seats. These front-of-cabin or exit row seats are
frequently held back for the company's most frequent flyers,
or offered at a small premium during reservation. The idea
that rows 6-12 warrant an extra $20 was entirely built on the
observation that consumers prefer to sit at the front of the air-
craft and are willing to pay (in cash, time, or points) to do so.

The Bar Brawl: Demonstrable Status

People are intrinsically competitive, though generally for different reasons and about different things. Some people are
motivated by money while others really care about being attractive. Some of us are status oriented while others primarily
want to be loved. While motivations may differ, the drive is
the same: everybody likes to win. And while acknowledging
this desire doesn't diminish our individualism, it does point
out an important truth: many of our behaviors can be manipulated to advance the cause of marketing.

Take the passive competition inherent in getting a drink at
a crowded bar on the weekend. The bar is packed—say, four
people deep—on top of those people who lucked into seating
on the few available stools. The objective is plain: get your
drinks and get back to your friends as quickly as possible. If
there is no specific line, you might have to muscle your way
between people and turn to the side. Once you are positioned,
you must establish eye contact with the bartender. Holding
money visibly in your hand is a subtle way of indicating that
you want service. You can't push people out of the way or call
out loudly. The bartender will refuse service if you break the
rules, and the bouncers will evict you.

Of course, there's a big social reward, waiting for you once you manage to bring your friends a fistful of drinks from a crowded bar: their appreciation and respect. Beyond the alcoholic buzz, that's the reinforcement we are most interested in seeking.

The bar game—like the coffee shop game—has levels. For customers who are friends with the bartender, the benefits are cheaper drinks and better service. For the regulars and those who tip well, less waiting time or free drinks are their reward. And their conditioning is strong and well warranted: research by liquor control company Capton shows that an estimated $7 billion is lost each year in the United States alone from bartenders overpouring, undercharging, or just offering free drinks. While some of these instances are honest mistakes, personal stories suggest that bartenders, like slot machines, know a thing or two about conditioned rewards. So, how can the bar itself exploit this game, already in play, instead of merely being the loser in the economic equation? How does the game go from passive to active? Interestingly, bars are highly evolved in how they think about status rewards.

VIP areas are the most obvious manifestation of status thinking in the beverage service industry. VIPs don't have to endure the same crowded bar experience, and the most effective VIP sections are those with the most visibility. Tables with "reserved" signs and dedicated waitstaff cause other patrons to wonder how they might achieve a comparable level of service. Do they need to pay more? Spend more time at the bar? Be famous? If a point system were put into play, perhaps clients would learn that by buying enough drinks, they could accrue points to win access to the VIP door, at which there is no waiting. And of course, drinks bartenders and servers fail to ring into the system would not earn points, thereby encouraging customers to insist that their order be correctly attributed.

Patrons who earn points through longevity might also receive free drinks, get entry into the VIP section, have less wait time at the bar, or gain something as simple as visibility on a leaderboard. More complex challenges such as answering trivia questions, participating in bar games, or bringing new people to the venue could substantially deepen the experience.

It's all about status and its display. Thus, the ways in which people engage in passive play—be it at a bar, a coffee shop, or in any other business model—can be used to a company's advantage, but only once the basic game rewards are out in the open.

The Components of Funware

As in a bar's VIP area, Starbucks coffee line, or subway battles, there are a number of key elements that signal and compose the games played all around us:

- *Status and Levels:* Status is an outward display of achievement. Levels are a convenient way to divide play into achievable subgames while also creating status shorthand. They are frequently interchangeable and invariably go hand-in-hand.
- *Points:* To keep track of how we're doing in a game, we need a scorekeeping system and comparison table, such as Facebook's friend count.
- *Rules:* Fighting for a rush hour seat on the subway or bus is a great example of a game that is played with clear (if unarticulated) rules. Without these structures, there would be chaos.
- *Demonstrability:* Sitting in a VIP section at a club would be a lot less fun if no one saw you there, wouldn't it?

Making all these components *demonstrable* is what gives marketers the power of status persuasion.

Through these elements, passive game-play occurs whether or not we care, understand, or see it happening. However, by recognizing these games for what they are—powerful indicators of the desires of their client base as well as shortcuts to putting *active games* into play—marketers can begin to work with these inexpensive, powerfully effective marketing tools.

Once we understand the components, our first challenge is to harness their power in the form of basic Funware designs that can be used to achieve marketing objectives. The first and simplest architecture is the *leaderboard* and its social networking context. Let's take a closer look at how comparing scores can be a game in itself.

Key Concepts:

- Passive games are different from active games in that most players don't even realize a game is being played.

- Demonstrable levels of play can be used by marketers to reward loyalty and encourage new users to join the loyalty game.

- Points provide the basic underpinning of scorekeeping, and social networking sites provide a unique opportunity to drive scoring behavior.

- Rules, whether obvious or not, are essential both for maintaining order and for effective Funware design.

- Success is much less interesting if it's not social and others don't see you win.

Social Networks and Leaderboards

Social Network Clutter

Before the popularity of social media sites like Facebook, MySpace, and Twitter took the business world by storm, most loyalty programs were merely a component of marketing campaigns designed to mesh with branding, direct marketing, and public relations. Other than those offered by the hospitality industry, loyalty programs rarely go beyond coffee punch cards, "buy-X-get-Y" systems, or simplistic rebate/point mechanisms like the Discover Card cash back scheme. In fact, customer loyalty is such a commoditized—and misunderstood—notion among marketers that a quick Google search for "loyalty programs" reveals that there are dozens of companies offering out-of-the-box solutions for as little as $29.95 per month. In fact, one prominent marketing textbook used at the MBA level devotes a scant two pages out of nearly a thousand pages of text to customer loyalty programs.

But in our "skip-the-commercials" instant gratification world filtered by "smart apps" like TiVo, consumers are increasingly unlikely to respond to the more traditional techniques used by marketers. Display advertising, direct marketing, and even high-level branding have been withering in effectiveness. Concurrently, the advertising and guerilla campaign markets on Facebook, MySpace, and Twitter continue to be nascent, offering little in the way of structured opportunities for marketers.

Since 2005, the combined effect of social media growth and the 2008 economic downturn on advertising budgets have been staggering. According to TNS Media Intelligence, total U.S. advertising spending has declined roughly 16 percent, or $23 billion since Facebook truly took the Internet by storm. That astonishing number is approximately equal to the total ad revenues of the entire newspaper industry. Some sectors have taken an even more powerful hit. According to *MediaDailyNews*, local advertising spending has declined 32 percent in that same time period, taking thousands of jobs and billions of dollars in value with it.

Meanwhile, Forrester Research predicts that interactive marketing spending will rise to nearly $54 billion by 2014. And the fastest growing segment within their analysis is Social Media, with a projected 34 percent CAGR from 2009 to 2014.

Social networking, it turns out, is both marketing's sickness—and its cure.

Marketing with Social Networks

At the core of marketing through social networking sites is the leaderboard, still the most effective tool for creating active game-play. The term itself, and its most commonly understood implementation, originates from sports (like golf, for example), where a publicly displayed board is used to help bystanders follow the action's progress. Similarly, one of the simplest ways to trigger the desire to engage, play, and win is to surface a leaderboard. The simple goal of risingup in the rankings is often enough of a motivator for players to start and continue playing.

Orkut: A Case Study in Leaderboard Effectiveness

Consider the example of Orkut, Google's proprietary social networking site. At the outset, the site's designers innocently displayed a simple country counter that showed the number of users from various nations who had registered to network. Seemingly out of nowhere, Brazilians took this as a challenge to their national pride. Dozens of blogs and meetups appeared

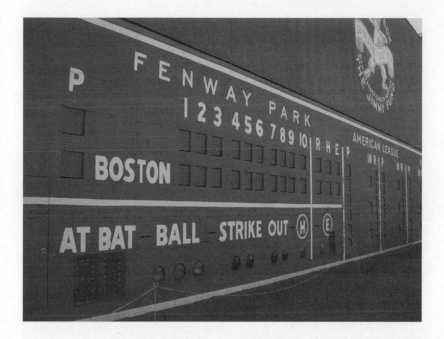

that encouraged people to sign up with a simple objective in mind: to push Brazil to the top of the country rankings. In fact, parties were held all over the country when its score beat that of the United States. Google never structured any challenges or prizes for the top country. This entire competition happened *spontaneously* in response to the mere existence of a leaderboard. Today, Brazil's number-one social network is Orkut, not Facebook.

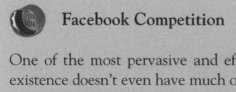

Facebook Competition

One of the most pervasive and effective leaderboards in existence doesn't even have much of a formal structure. All 100 million–plus Facebook profiles have a little "score"

(continued)

(*continued*)

below them: the number of friends each person has. This statistic is so meaningful in the Facebook environment that it's displayed whether or not you are officially "friends" with the other person. No *active* game exists; there is no prize for the individual with the highest friend count. However, the prominent placement of an individual's number of friends—even to people who may be casually browsing a person's profile —creates an esoteric leaderboard of sorts. Most people are aware of their friend count, and most of their friends are aware of their *friends'* friend count. They likely know which of their friends have the highest number and how many friends they need to acquire in order to have as many or more. People are *passively* keeping a kind of ranked list, and while the competition may be unintentional, it is most assuredly taking place.

However, in the absence of a formal leaderboard for friend (or follower) count, Facebook and other similar social networks miss the opportunity to *motivate* users to take specific actions. For example, if an individual on Facebook knew that he or she stood at number 11 among the most popular people in a group of friends, he or she might become interested in maintaining that ranking and might even be motivated to go out and meet new people in order to break into the Top 10.

Funware at Work: Facebook Friend Games

Most marketers think of Facebook games as stand-alone applications they develop to promote a brand within Facebook. But given the pervasiveness of the passive friends game on Facebook, perhaps there is more opportunity to innovate.

Consider the power of a marketing offering that would raise a Facebook user's number of friends (and their passive leaderboard position). This would be especially appealing if the new friends are high quality. Perhaps you can offer online friendships with celebrities as part of a campaign (instead of obtaining mere endorsements). Or perhaps a contest that rewards lucky winners with friendships with entire sporting teams or famous supermodels would be a good fit with your brand and consumer interest.

As evidenced by top-ranked Facebook apps like "Hot or Not" and "Texas Hold 'Em Poker," users frequently value new social connections as much as any other reward. By making these connections explicit, your brand can leverage the Facebook game in spectacular new ways.

No News *Isn't* Good News

Let's now take a closer look at the opposite and even more important case: the Facebook user with 125 friends. According to Facebook's internal statistics, this "player" is perfectly average. But because there is no leaderboard to consult, such players have no idea whether they are popular. The only method of measuring this is by heuristic observation of the number of friends *their* friends seem to have.

However, this approach is likely to immediately introduce a negatively reinforcing bias for these players. Because more social and more densely "friended" users are more likely to update their status, upload pictures, and comment on the site, the standard player may begin to think that 125 is far short of the average number of friends. While this sense of "failure" can be invigorating for a highly competitive person, it may have the effect of depressing "play" in the context of the site for the average user. In other words, such players might think of themselves as losers and stop play altogether.

All this could be resolved by using a simple leaderboard. By displaying the status of all members in the context of their friends—as well as the site's other members—even the most lax of players might find themselves substantially emboldened to become more involved. And because the friend count cannot be hidden, players could even be proud of their perfectly average stats. In fact, some motivation may lie in knowing that adding four more friends will allow even a standard player to overtake two other friends and enter the Top 20 within his or her social circle. This kind of *dynamic challenge* can be designed in software to constantly encourage users to invest and reinvest in your Funware.

In short, people like to keep score—even when there's nothing to win. The leaderboard is a critical tool in making that a reality. While Facebook and Twitter have only begun to scratch the surface of effective uses of leaderboards, marketers and managers have been deploying this Funware tactic for decades.

Leaderboards in Business

Leaderboards have been visible, if less explicit, for many years in a business context. After all, "Employee of the Month" signage is a simple way to reward and encourage staff members' excellence. Competitive sales graphs showing the performance of various reps, branches, or divisions are commonly displayed in corporate settings as well. But while the HR value of the leaderboard is quite well understood (as it is in competitive sports), it is also an extraordinarily powerful and cost-effective tool for affecting user behavior.

The Jigsaw Example

Jigsaw.com is a business-to-business marketplace for contact information that has successfully employed Funware and a leaderboard to encourage consumer data sharing. Essentially a "wallet" for virtual business cards, Jigsaw allows its users to both upload and download full contact information for business leads across a wide range of industries and companies. The site charges a minimum $20 monthly subscription fee for access to the contact information directory, and more than 100,000 users are currently active subscribers.

Although the idea behind the Web site is somewhat controversial (after all, you can upload anyone's contact information—with or without their consent), it's a simple and compelling notion. While it would be virtually impossible to create an up-to-date database of contact information for more than 16 million professionals in a cost-effective manner, Jigsaw relies on its users to upload the business cards they gather at tradeshows and conferences and through their social networks.

Initially, the company paid users as much as $1 per card for uploading third-party contacts. However, with only $18 million in capital raised through 2009, Jigsaw couldn't possibly have paid for the upload and maintenance of every person in the database. So, the designers turned to Funware for the answer. They created and deployed a points-based economy that rewards users for the actions they take within the site. Now Jigsaw users can earn points for uploading, subscribing, and inviting friends. In this way, users can redeem their points for bonuses above and beyond merely their subscription level.

Perhaps Jigsaw's most compelling Funware strategy has been its leaderboard—a place where users can compare their performance with others in the network. In fact, the company offers leaderboards for each of the core activities it seeks to promote: New Contacts Added, Contacts Updated, Referrers, and Wikis (notes). These leaderboards, along with the challenges, levels, badges, and points that they summarize, have enabled the company to move from *cash* compensation to *virtual* compensation. This approach eliminates huge costs, results in substantial advantages for the company's competitive space, and encourages users to take actions that directly benefit the company without realizing any obvious reward themselves.

For some users, their ranking on the leaderboard *is* their reward. For others—and possibly, most important, for marketers—the greatest power of leaderboards is that they distinctly indicate that some kind of game is being played. They reveal the existence of a ranking mechanism, signal a

point system, and suggest the presence of rules for ways to garner those points. They are an essential part of the puzzle in game-based marketing.

Correctly Using Leaderboards

A sign at a construction site reads "190 Days Since Our Last Accident." At first glance, a notice like this one may not reveal itself as a leaderboard. However, it clearly suggests that some scorekeeping is taking place, even if each person who reads it has a different idea of what "win" means in this context. For some observers, anything less than 1,000 safe days would signify a problem, while others might be satisfied with seeing 30.

The purpose of such a sign is, plainly, to encourage safety on job sites. However, the efficacy of a negative behavior leaderboard is decidedly up for debate, and a narrowly defined mechanism lacks many of the characteristics we'd expect to see in a commercial setting for Funware. We're apt to ask some tough questions when we look closely at the design of this leaderboard:

- What defines an *accident*?
- How much control does one individual have over the *possibility* of an accident?
- Does the sign *itself* motivate the workers?
- Is it intended to encourage the site managers who have little to do with the jobs themselves—and therefore the job site's ultimate safety?
- To whom does the responsibility for failure fall?

Now, in order to build a leaderboard for a construction site using effective game methodology, a site manager might have to do a fair bit more work. The foreman may be required to track *every* safety measure that *each* worker proactively took into his or her own hands instead of just measuring each "safe day" that passes as a data point. Every time someone puts on a hard hat when walking onto the site, every time someone calls a work stoppage for an unsafe activity, and every time safe behaviors are maintained, points earned could ultimately be made visible on a different sort of leaderboard—one that focuses on *safe* behaviors rather than *dangerous* ones. While this leaderboard may seem like substantially more work to maintain, it would also achieve a far more effective—not to mention *safer*—outcome.

In addition to having an internal leaderboard, it might be interesting to connect this safety scheme across various job sites, comparing the safety culture of specific players, locations, companies, cities, counties—even states—so that maximum opportunities would exist for players to win. This might lead to a more tangible and measurably positive effect on safety culture in comparison with the sign approach. Tax breaks, faster permitting, and other rewards might incentivize the executive level to ensure safer working conditions in the construction field across the board.

Although it probably doesn't come as a surprise, very little data is available for measuring how effective the "days since" approach can be. However, we know from game industry experience that this design lacks positive reinforcement—a critical element of Funware design, and of which marketers should be keenly aware. Simply put, a well-designed Funware application should reinforce positive behaviors early and often, ensuring that consumers are engaged and excited from the get-go. While it may seem patronizing, there is no upper limit to the amount of positive reinforcement game players seek. Remember: what seems insincere from a design perspective rarely translates as such in actual situations.

> Construction safety is big business. In the United States, although construction workers make up only 8 percent of the workforce, 22 percent of job-related fatalities occur in construction, making it the most dangerous industry sector in the country. So, the effect of the leaderboard and the associated Funware that is used in this sector has the potential to substantially improve—and *lengthen*—the lives of tens of thousands of workers.

Points Proxy: Masking and Directing Behaviors

One of the things that Funware does very effectively is to combine an enjoyable pastime like play with another, often less enjoyable activity. By collecting points or achieving status, the very personal sense of accomplishment inherent in this powerful combination can lead to an outcome greater than the sum of its parts.

Of course, leaderboards aren't an across-the-board panacea for all marketing woes. What happens when privacy issues conflict with the transparency that these tools offer? For example, if the government were to use Funware intended to encourage Americans to increase their savings rates, it would likely begin by giving people incentives to save more. People might be awarded points, levels, badges, and possibly even cash and tax rewards for saving money (the latter already exist in the United States in the form of 401K and IRA programs).

Whatever technique is first chosen, one of the most powerful tools to encourage this behavior would be a leaderboard. Allowing citizens to compare themselves with their friends, coworkers, family members, and neighbors would likely engender positive reinforcement behavior that just might begin to curb our culture of excess. However compelling, this social energy might indirectly expose some uncomfortable information, like the amount of money people have. This carries a grave, though not insurmountable, risk.

In another Funware example, a gym decides to create a weight loss game for its patrons. Obviously, exposing a person's weight on a public display board would be a sticking point for many players. However, by devising clever point systems intended to mask the underlying value of those points, the leaderboard can prevail.

For example, points could be awarded for the core behavior as well as for ancillary or correlate behaviors. So, to encourage thrift among Americans, the government might award points for the *relative* dollars saved (in terms of comparison with overall wealth or previous saving habits, for example) rather than just recognizing absolute savings. In the case of weight loss, people might be rewarded for literal pounds lost as well as given "kickers" or accelerants based on relative amounts (a 20 percent bonus when your weight hits the target, for example). Although these kinds of designs can be more complex (and similarly opaque), they increase the likelihood that users will participate in a highly personal game.

Moreover, multifactor point schemes have benefits that go beyond merely hiding awkward information; they also allow the designer to encourage many different kinds of behavior under a single aegis. Points for both direct and relative activities as well as for accomplishing key objectives can ultimately be combined to produce a *score*. It then becomes the job of the leaderboard to simplify that score into a ranking, using various devices, that makes it easy to understand how challenging—and rewarding—it may be to excel.

Wal-Mart and the Theory of Relativism

Relative leaderboards are the standard method used in *social ranking systems*. They are incredibly well suited for socially networked contexts and are becoming the norm across all comparative tools. While it was impossible to do so during the mechanical scoreboard days, we're now able to produce instant digital leaderboards that are capable of showing users their score and rank relative to:

- the 10 players above and below them,
- others of similar skill levels,
- others in their same geographical area, and
- their "friends" (using the social graph inherent in Facebook or MySpace).

Relative leaderboards allow businesses to show active and prospective players a competitive view that creates the maximum sense of accomplishment for a particular individual at that moment. This variety of leaderboards within the same application raises consumer interest as well as the likelihood that new players will want to join the game.

Wal-Mart's Facebook application, "Saving Money and Living Better," provides a clear illustration of a relative leaderboard in play. The premise of the game is to find deals in the real world that players post to their Facebook pages. A player earns points for each post and every deal he or she follows. In this way, relative incentives are meted out for all critical behaviors: discovery, promotion, and qualification.

Wal-Mart's tool is designed in such a way that when players click on the leaderboard button, the first leaderboard they see is one in which they look good but where the encouragement to proceed (and win) is obvious. The second leaderboard compares them with their friends to provide a more meaningful contrast and a straightforward platform for promotion of the application through the leaderboard. The third view is optional and consists of the traditional list of Top 10 players.

Keeping Hope Alive—Optimizing for Winnability

While the biggest problem with Facebook and Twitter's point scheme is the absence of a leaderboard—(and therefore any kind of guiding structure), the most significant danger in an explicit leaderboard design occurs when new players think winning is *impossible*. This is especially true of a game with a point system that has a lot of zeros; the visual deterrent of large numbers might have the unintentional effect of discouraging prospective players. It's akin to what happens when you walk up to a pinball or video game to find a top score of 300 million. Even if the point system measures activities in the most inflationary way possible, the casual observer has no effective way of knowing how difficult it might be to reach that goal.

Conversely, awarding users huge amounts of points for achieving basic objectives is a powerful motivator—one that is frequently practiced in electronic game design. In this regard, balance is vital. Many designers agree that the right point scheme tracks closely to a player's perceived value of money in the real world. For example, the denomination of currency profoundly affects people's conception of big numbers and small numbers. In other words, value often pivots on the number of zeros in a national currency.

Consider the currencies of the United States and Zimbabwe. Until redenomination in February 2009, $1 USD was worth $1 trillion Zimbabwean dollars. So whereas one million in the United States is typically perceived as a large number, in Zimbabwe one billion is considered a small number. In the United States, one hundred points for completing a simple activity feels substantial while in Zimbabwe, multiplying the point scheme by 100,000 (or 1,000,000) would improve face validity.

Leaderboard Levels

No boxing manager would ever pit a bantamweight against a featherweight or a cruiserweight against a heavyweight. These fighters are separated into categories because, over time, it has become clear that the bigger guys tend to knock out the little guys.

When there are substantial differences that prevent people from being effectively compared with one another, we must create separate buckets to compensate. In a game measuring weight loss or savings rates, for example, the meaning of achievement may be dramatically different from person to person: one player's goal might be to lose 100 pounds, another person's might simply be 5 or 10.

Or consider the frequent flier who averages 100,000 miles a year. That player might consider a stretch goal of 150,000 miles to be a reasonable objective in a challenge. On the other hand, for a player who flies 5,000 miles a year, 150,000 miles is an absolutely unimaginable amount of flying. Not only is it

30 times his or her base amount of flying, numerically, it's simply a nonstarter.

Put another way: If winning a game required people to turn purple and fly by flapping their arms, they probably wouldn't bother playing either. So, pitting these two players against each other on one continuous leaderboard would have the effect of making the 5,000-mile-a-year traveler feel like he or she shouldn't even bother playing the game, and the 150,000-mile flyer would never even know that the other person was playing.

Clever design separates out people of radically different levels before displaying the leaderboard information in an effective way. Relative leaderboards and associated levels are two ways to effectively rank players and share information with them. A third method is to use graphic elements that signify secondary leaderboard characteristics such as icons that represent various achievements paralleling the base score.

Leaderboards: The Top 10

Despite—or perhaps *because of*—their simplicity, leaderboards are a highly effective and affordable way to create a Funware experience around a business objective. While it benefits from a comprehensive, underlying point system, the leaderboard itself can have the effect of catalyzing a game experience just by virtue of being visible to the target consumer. We are all drawn to the scoreboard, and within seconds we analyze its meaning, readily intuiting both the existence of a game and the probability of winning.

This is why it's critical to design the leaderboard with great sensitivity to both the social and psychological factors that affect our desire to play. Remain conscientious in terms of the sociability of rankings, a belief in winnability, and the leaderboard's ability to channel an innate desire to win in a positive rather than negative way.

Similarly, you can design a point scheme of almost limitless complexity that underlies the leaderboard. It must, however, ensure the privacy of its players, maintain the opacity of scoring when dealing with sensitive subjects, and provide multiple opportunities for users to compete and win even if their notion of winning is radically different. And leaderboards and point systems need not be 100 percent literal. Often, the game is as important as the product itself, and disconnecting the two can work wonders in a complex environment.

As a cost-effective method for creating a gamelike experience, very few tools are as potentially valuable as the leaderboard. In fact, experience has shown that the leaderboard is generally the best initial Funware approach for most types of marketing. Even in the absence of a thoughtful point system, users will pay closer attention to the game's design when a leaderboard is presented. Thereafter, by building out the other components of a Funware architecture—like points, levels, badges, and challenges—game mechanics can provide a greater depth of experience for users, allowing you to maximize the marketing effect of Funware in your endeavor.

The Future of Fun: The Incongruous Leaderboard

Leaderboards don't always need to be literal in order to be effective. While we discuss the importance of a comprehensive point system extensively throughout this book, the leaderboard used to reinforce and engage user behavior need not relate directly to a business's principal objective.

(continued)

(*continued*)

For example, a nutritional drink company might deploy a Funware application that includes a leaderboard that's focused on getting patients in an assisted living home to keep their weight up. By simply keeping the system updated with the patients' weekly weight gains or losses, the leaderboard would adjust accordingly. Although the company would not reward residents directly for drinking their beverage, the leaderboard itself is both practical and powerful as a game-centric branding opportunity, encouraging consumption in a powerful, if indirect way. Thus the brand benefits from a positive association with a healthful activity while engaging players with the power of Funware. The opportunities are virtually limitless once you transcend literality in business game design.

Key Concepts:

- Social networks provide an unparalleled opportunity to market using game mechanics.
- Leaderboards are often the best initial Funware mechanics to use as they are cost-effective and easy for users to understand.
- Even simple leaderboards like the "friend count" on Facebook can have a profound effect on user behavior.
- Leaderboards can and should show many different kinds of rankings, including socially relative ones.
- Fine-tuning a leaderboard to convey challenge and winnability is key.
- In combination with a well-designed point system, even sensitive topics can be tracked on a leaderboard.

Funware Mechanics: Points and Beyond

I n 1897, the Sperry and Hutchinson (S&H) Company began selling stamps to retailers. S&H Green Stamps became one of the most expansive and longest-running loyalty programs in history. The earning premise was simple: buy a specified dollar amount of product at a participating retailer, and receive stamps.

The company's retailers ranged from gas stations to supermarkets, but principally consisted of purveyors of everyday goods. Once collected, the stamps were redeemable for items (including housewares and gifts) sold at Green Stamp stores and through catalogs. Hitting its pinnacle of popularity in the 1960s, the company claims to have at one time printed three times as many stamps as the U.S. Postal Service.

S&H Green Stamps was a scheme that perfectly illustrated a simple point system at work. Each stamp represented a point, and value was assigned to the points by the Green Stamp company and its participating retailers. Consumers understood the value of a stamp only through product-specific redemption rates within the catalog itself. Participation was a no-brainer for customers; they were going to buy those things anyway, so why not get a seemingly free reward? Like any simple incentive scheme—such as the buy-10-get-1-free cards offered by local coffee shops— there was no signup form, demographic survey, 12-digit number, or username-password combination required to join.

By the 1990s, S&H had greatly contracted in the face of stiff competition from more enmeshed and holistic Funware offered principally by FFPs. S&H's failure to understand that the increased engagement of FFPs would erode its core business is an object lesson in how the power of fun to motivate and inspire can be overlooked. After all, most FFP miles are substantially more difficult to redeem than S&H Green Stamps ever were—and retail is much more accessible than air travel. So, if it weren't for the rise of fun, perhaps today's traveler might earn Greenpoints instead of miles with every flight!

Making Points the Point

The purpose of a point system like S&H Green Stamps is to allow marketers to easily incentivize user behavior with maximum flexibility. By shifting reward tracking from simple relationships ("buy 10 coffees, get 1 free") to abstract numbering systems, you can introduce a limitless variety of incentive-reward relationships. In this way, marketers can easily create promotions and deflate/inflate the currency at will, moving consumer preference and behavior with a simple switch.

This abstraction hides the shifting value of points from users in a way that is generally positive for your Funware efforts. When the ratio of action to reward is very obvious, making changes to the schema often comes with substantial user pushback. This is the reason why the basic reward in FFPs— the domestic US free ticket—has remained at 25,000 miles for nearly 20 years, while every other reward has become substantially more expensive in that time. Since the most popular flight redemption is the domestic award, a change in its value would disproportionately agitate users and affect the marketing comparison between programs. So, by leaving it alone, and radically devaluing other rewards, FFP designers can meet their business objectives without substantial customer pushback. However, it places a monetary value on those points.

In the same vein, imagine switching "buy 10 coffees get one free" to "buy 12 coffees get one free," and the decrease invalue of the abstracted points becomes immediately obvious. Now, if ten coffees were worth 100 points instead of coffee, what those 100 points can "buy" may fluctuate along with the marketing goals of the company without impacting the game in a way that overtly affects play.

Most businesses engaging in Funware issue points concurrent with a base activity. For example, "Earn one point per mile flown or dollar spent." Of course, if products are sold in units, such as gallons or liters of gas, points may work better when assigned by units sold. Within a game or Funware context, points can also be earned by taking actions solely within the virtual world. For example, "Solve this puzzle and get 10 points" or "Invite friends and receive 20 points per new registrant."

Point Mechanics and Branding

Naming the point system is an important part of the branding exercise of a loyalty program. Most companies tack the word "point" or "mile" onto their principal brand, while many loyalty programs are marketed under a subsidiary identity from the parent company. Online games, in contrast, tend to prefer "gold," "coins," or "points" as naming systems. Often, the lack of interesting names (and neologisms) for loyalty points is a result of initial insecurity about their future and the desire to make the program more obvious to consumers. Regardless of the path you choose, making some clear decisions early in the process will help consumers align behind a common language for your program.

Similar considerations exist for the tracking of points. Of course, the S&H idea of printing actual stamps, binding books in which to paste them, and stocking stores in which to redeem them seems complicated at best and antiquated at worst. However, through a combination of technology and good design, we can now do more with points—and do it more cheaply—than ever before.

A number of third-party technology companies offer software solutions to help manage point systems. Even building a management tool is not terribly complex or overwhelmingly costly. As with most marketing efforts, the design considerations, such as the virtual economy and its balance, are substantially more involved than the technology required to execute them.

Virtual Economics

Critically, a point system is better deployed within the context of a well-rounded virtual economy. While the designers of most Funware applications have less responsibility than a central bank, their job is actually quite similar: to match the demand and supply of money as symmetrically as possible.

Simply put, a good point system is based on two elements: an *earning component* and a *redemption component*. Luckily for most of us, although it sounds complex, great Funware design does not require a degree in economics.

Funware at Play—RecycleBank

In a program similar to S&H Green Stamps, RecycleBank offers a point system to encourage its users to recycle. In partnership with municipalities and consumers themselves, RecycleBank's premise is that the application of simple Funware mechanics (points and redemptions) will encourage more users to recycle. Users may redeem their points by shopping with one of the company's participating retailers, including Dunkin' Donuts, IKEA, CVS, Coca-Cola, Evian, and Whole Foods Market.

So far, the program has been a huge success. The company claims to have doubled recycling rates in its member cities and diverted more than three million trees worth of paper goods and 194 million gallons of oil (equivalents in plastic and other materials) from landfills.

Virtual Currency

Virtual currencies aren't anything new, and neither is the temptation to use them. Kids have been stealing from the *Monopoly* till since Parker Brothers first dyed their $20s mint green and their $500s golden orange. Of course, everyone understood that outside the context of *Monopoly*, those bills, square "property" titles, and bright red hotels could not be redeemed for real cash. But within the experience of the game, people fought to land on Boardwalk before it was owned and to stay off it afterward. Enterprising young players traded properties and sold real estate to each other "off book." The bottom line is that *Monopoly* money has value in the context of the game because players *agree* that it does.

Generally, this shared value of money is the concept that also underlies the real currency market. Once people no longer believe that a particular currency is useful, massive devaluation occurs. In the virtual world however, if everyone agrees that a currency is useful and its underlying experience *fun*, then perceived value grows.

While maintaining an enjoyable experience is principally a function of the overall Funware design, the currency element actually contributes directly to a sense of enjoyment.

Denominations are more engaging as they get larger; for example, it's much more fun to win a million points than 100 points, even if they have the same redemption value. And, if properly designed, the players of your Funware experience will have lots of great things to redeem them for.

Real-World Value versus Virtual Value

Airlines do not trade miles for cash. However, there are third-party sellers who will buy and sell miles with real-world money (despite the explicit rules of the program that prohibit these sales). The fact that a real-world market has evolved from a corporate loyalty program makes sense when you consider that the value of the miles often translates into real-world status, rewards, and sometimes travel.

Even more surprising than cash redemptions for frequent flyer miles is that some online games, such as *World of Warcraft*, have thousands of unofficial Web sites solely devoted to the selling of virtual gold using real-world currency. The virtual gold in *World of Warcraft* (its point system) has *no official real-world value*. And yet people continue to spend real money to buy it. This fact incidentally gives *World of Warcraft* gold a real-world value of sorts. Of course, this outcome was not intended by the game's designers, though it proves that people will apply value to virtual goods if the game they are playing is meaningful enough to them.

Marketers therefore need not give people real-world goods and rewards in exchange for real-world expenditures if a sufficiently vibrant virtual economy exists. Thus, there is another incentive to create a great Funware experience for users that includes virtual rewards: a well-functioning virtual economy can reduce marketing and promotion costs by half or more.

Creating an Easy and Effective Virtual Economy

As a marketer, you can create a simple virtual economy without having a PhD in economics. Start by tying it directly to the activity you want to incentivize (usually purchases). Then, offer rewards to users that they might find appealing. The critical piece is to intermediate these steps using a virtual currency of your own definition so that you can easily adjust redemption levels (costs) up or down as necessary.

As your virtual economy picks up steam, you can begin to offer more options for earning and redeeming points, taking care to balance the demand against supply. Create relationships with business partners to offer meaningful prizes, and focus on the excitement associated with the process of earning and redeeming. By introducing experiences that mimic gameplay, your consumers become *players* and simple interactions with your business become fun. Over time, well designed Funware will attract users to rewards that are entirely virtual—items with no real-world redemption value whatsoever that come at no additional cost (once designed) to your business. Incorporating these rewards into the architecture of the game at the outset is valuable.

A good example of this is Mycokerewards.com. Coca-Cola consumers earn points by entering codes from bottle caps into the Web site and creating an account. Points can then be redeemed for physical (and some virtual) merchandise. Crucially, the real-world redemption options are given top billing to encourage users to join the program—trips, electronics and Coca-Cola products, for example. In this way, the real-world rewards are a central part of the marketing scheme. However, if Mycokerewards.com were able to shift the goals of its players toward its virtual redemption items—including better positioning within the game, virtual experiences and virtual prizes—the social and brand effectiveness would upswing substantially. As is the case with branded merchandise rewards, the prizes are in many cases like a badge. Players who earn the rewards will demonstrably wear the logo and even sing the praises of the brand or product, signaling their accomplishments to others and reinforcing the value of the game itself.

Badging Players

Whether in Mycokerewards.com or *World of Warcraft*, players must attach meaning to game mechanics in order for the game to be validated. Badges are therefore useful since they provide players an opportunity to display their accomplishments inside and outside the Funware itself. Often represented visually, badges show that players have completed specific tasks. The badge's value is a powerful and fundamentally social game mechanic. While society generally discourages personal claims of accomplishment like bragging, badges allow boasting without being obvious. They are the ultimate passive-aggressive status symbols since, of course, a badge that no one can see has limited value.

The term itself may conjure up images of the Boy Scouts of America. Merit badges, for example, are embedded in popular lore; scouts are awarded badges for completing any one of hundreds of challenges laid out by the organization. In the real world of the Boy Scouts, badges are patches bearing images of the completed task, which are displayed by being sewn onto the uniform.

In a more contemporary sense, it has been repeatedly shown that people will compete for visible badges on social networking sites. Employing Facebook apps that offer ways for users to display their accomplishments is an example of an easy and cost-efficient way to "badge" your players. Given the advances of Facebook and other social networking platforms, virtual badges may already be more valuable to most users than the physical equivalent. (After all, it might be prohibitive to sew a literal badge onto a cashmere sweater.)

A bumper sticker, for example, that serves as a real-world badge does not lack value. "Parent of a Fifth Grade Honor Student" is an easy and cost-effective form of badging, however the lack of clarity about who will see the bumper sticker (and whether or not the driver of the the car matters to those that do) reduces its value. When a badge is placed on a Facebook profile, it is almost guaranteed that the people who see the badge are socially relevant to the user.

Of course, there's no downside to making physical badges, especially if your users pay for them. Allowing your players to use their points for real-world badges is merely another opportunity to build a *sink*, or redemption channel, for your virtual currency. And redeeming points for branded merchandise is a time-honored tradition that also ensures the propagation of the sponsoring brand; every time that T-shirt is worn, others see the identity.

The bottom line: the more meaningful ways there are to spend points, the more valuable those points become.

T-Shirt Giveaways, Funware Style

Consider the difference between the standard marketing approach to a promotional shirt offer and a Funware-centric view. In a normal marketing program, shirts are given away to customers at events and through promotions and are designed mostly to expose others to the brand. But a Funware-centric marketing campaign would view the shirts as an opportunity to both brand the company *and* engender loyalty in the wearer.

At your next shirt event, why not create three different kinds of shirts of increasing scarcity? Invite a reputable designer to design them, and offer them as part of a small series of contests or promotions. Motivated winners of a limited edition T-shirt with a famous signature or cool bit of graffiti art will be likely to wear the item frequently and evangelize the fact that they won it. This kind of enhanced engagement costs you very little but creates excitement and engenders loyalty among your user base.

Newbie Badges

Most modern games begin by offering players a badge early on. This quick reinforcement creates a positive feedback loop and shows how to earn badges and view them later. In many traditional games, this first reward comes in the form of a *newbie badge*.

When new players enter the game world, a simple and easy-to-accomplish task should be set before them. "Invite three friends to join" or "complete your profile now" are two such challenges. By incentivizing this behavior with a reward, a player is more likely to engage in the game immediately. Positive reinforcement should happen early and often, and providing badges is a great, low-cost way of doing so.

Trophy Rooms

Some games offer trophy rooms wherein the accomplishments of players and their competition are displayed. This application allows users to look back over their game experience and to see what opportunities lie ahead. Although trophy rooms do not tend to be common in most Funware applications, they can be a powerful tool for your brand. A virtual display of accomplishments is always motivational and is arguably more sociable than displaying a trophy on a shelf in the living room.

Building Levels

Imagine that oil and gas supplier Chevron has decided to build an effective Funware loyalty program based around a virtual economy. Instinctively, the first reward the company is apt to consider offering its customers would be free gas. However, since the focus of this book is on saving money—not giving it away—let's consider what else Chevron could do in order to keep its virtual economy *virtual*.

On a social networking site like Facebook, Chevron might offer its players a virtual gas tank to display on their home page. Every time the player buys gas for their real-world car at Chevron, the virtual tank fills. To add more depth to the game, Chevron might consider allowing their consumer to create vehicular avatars in any style they wish. Every real life gas purchase correlates to a gas purchase for their virtual Lamborghini. Prizes, again, both virtual—such as a souped-up engine—and real-world—like a better fitting gas cap—redeemed using points, should be designed to badge the player. The color of the virtual car, for example, might correlate to real-world and virtual tasks completed. Levels guide longer-term objectives that motivate players to continue playing in an effort to reach a higher status. While standalone challenges, contests, or sweepstakes are useful for creating short-term alignment, levels help orient motivation beyond a short cycle of reward. Levels are things you strive for, and they mark progress throughout an experience. As such, they produce important psychological rewards that should be leveraged by smart marketers.

In the Boy Scouts, collecting badges helps boys achieve new levels. The Eagle Scouts, for example, require the acquisition of 21 merit badges as well as the completion of an extensive service project. By establishing a relationship between challenges, badges, and levels, the Boy Scouts have built one of the most successful leveling systems to date.

Any good marketing game must have similarly achievable and definitive levels. Taking into account the strengths and weaknesses of levels, a good game designer will choose to implement a model that will encourage long-term game involvement over the largest possible demographic and will continue to grow.

Leveling Up and Out

In most games, if you can beat the competition at the final level offered by the designer, you effectively win the game. Most successful interactive entertainment products continue to expand their offerings after the game has been released in order to provide additional levels for top players. These *expansion packs* or *sequels* have the benefit of extending the franchise and keeping players interested.

But some level systems don't have a natural point of expansion or offer this kind of option to players. The Boy Scouts, it would seem, have a natural end point: high school graduation. However, even the Boy Scouts have managed to expand their leveling system. Once a participant has completed Eagle Scout training, he or she can continue to grow within the system. For every 10 merit badges an Eagle Scout obtains, he receives a Palm award. Three such awards exist, culminating at the Gold Palm. Scouts may continue to ascend the ranks as junior advisors and beyond. After high school, paid positions in the Boy Scouts are similarly ranked all the way through district, regional, and national positions.

Additionally, scouts are rewarded in other contexts that exist regardless of rank. Religious and social awards can also be garnered during tenure in the Boy Scouts. By creating so many impressive levels of advancement as well as opportunities surrounding forward momentum, the Boy Scouts have created a virtually limitless cycle of striving and achievement.

America's Army

The U.S. military has one of the most recognizable systems of levels and badges. Although cryptic to the average civilian, every aspect of military dress and communication style is thoughtfully connected to a status marker. So, it probably comes as no surprise that the military has developed one of the most popular and interesting games of all time. *America's Army* is a fascinating case study that involves the use of game mechanics and Funware to achieve an impossible marketing coup: make one of the most challenging jobs in the world seem approachable and help lay the groundwork for a multi-billion dollar recruitment effort.

Col. Casey Wardynski created *America's Army* in order to communicate army career opportunities to young Americans. As director of the U.S. Army's Office of Economic and Man-power Analysis and the father of two boys, Wardynski inti-mately understands how game design and mechanics speak directly to his target audience. *America's Army* engages play-ers in an online army experience. Through the completion of tasks, players rise in rank within the virtual gaming system, which includes complex narrative threads. For example, if you complete the game's real-world based CPR simulation training, you can earn the Medic badge and unlock special virtual capability (and status).

The game's social components are also quite powerful. Play-ers group themselves into platoons as self-selected teams to guide play, and rank is similarly established. The social and narrative components of *America's Army*—buoyed by the com-plex badging and ranking architecture—have brought millions of players into a profound and satisfying game experience.

For Wardynski, the development of *America's Army* solved two major marketing problems for the military. In the 1990s, a steady economy led to a drop-off in army recruits. At the same time, the cost of cutting through the media clutter was increasing, making it progressively more difficult for the army to get its message across. What was needed was a tool that would allow the organization to communicate directly with its prospective customers: teenage recruit candidates.

"So, it popped into [my] mind," explained Wardynski during an extensive interview at his West Point offices, "Is there some way to package the army in a virtual experience that could be delivered directly to a household?"

This is the simple idea that became a smashing success.

America's Army is one of the most powerful non-draft recruitment tools in history. It has been played over 20 million times on an annual budget of less than $3 million per year. Perhaps even more important for the army's reach-based campaign, 26 percent of all men in America between the ages of 13 and 25 have played the game.

Defining and Meeting Goals

When building Funware, knowing the *goal* of the game is critically important to its design. One of Wardynski's crucial framing decisions in the development of *America's Army* was that the goal of the game would *not* be to directly recruit soldiers. "Our objective was decision space," he said. "If [the army] is not even in your decision space, forget recruits. How do I get into a kid's decision space?"

This choice was particularly interesting. A gamelike *America's Army* could easily have implemented a direct-response mechanism for new recruit prospecting; it could have even launched with a required registration step. However, the goal was to raise awareness and create an opportunity for the army's direct sales force (its recruiters) to more easily capitalize on growing consumer interest. And, in this way, it was a resounding success. A solid majority of players of

America's Army report adding the army to their list of career options post–high school. Wardynski pointed out that while traditional advertising can succeed in informing the public about a product, a game's power lies in its experience. "To her dying day, my grandmother thought I marched around all day," Wardynski laughed. "We're trying to communicate an answer to the question, 'What is it to be a soldier?'"

The simultaneous economic goal was an equally amazing success. The army pays between $2 and $8 per hour to reach consumers through television commercials. *America's Army* achieves that same branding effect for a scant 22 cents.

Funware at Play: A Closer Look at *America's Army*

Col. Casey Wardynski, architect of the successful *America's Army* game, sat down with the authors of *Game-Based Marketing* at his West Point office for an interview about key design considerations in making a fantastically successful marketing game. The following is an excerpt and the complete interview, including video, can be found at funwareblog.com:

Game-Based Marketing (**GBM**): We believe pretty fully that no matter what your business objective, fun needs to be the first consideration. Would you agree?

Colonel Wardynski (**CW**): Right. There's no point in [playing a game] if it's not fun—even if fun and the army aren't [traditionally] supposed to go together . . . .

GBM: What were some early thoughts about the design of *America's Army*?

CW: We looked at the games that were working; [for our demographic] they are first person, like the world of a soldier. It's not a real-time strategy game, which is what we had been envisioning up to that point: the world of the big shots looking down on the icons moving round. A single human can do anything in the virtual world whereas a platoon or a battalion or brigade really can't do many things. A division is not going to swim a river, swim an ocean, or fly.

GBM: Can you tell us about your job in the army?

CW: The job I have in the Department of Defense was created by General Thurman way back in 1982 when the army was failing to recruit volunteers. We are a direct support entity to the army. My charter is really one line: Help senior leaders create the army of the future.

GBM: Is your background in economics?

CW: We call it economics, but it's really public policy—it's statistics, economics, and behavioral science—applied economics. I don't go off and create any theory; I look at the body of theory that [already] exists and apply it to governmental problems. I'm an associate professor of economics at West Point, so that makes me an economist.

GBM: Why create a game?

CW: We realized we could lick a big economic problem, which is a boring term called *intermediation*. The media acts as an intermediary, or middle-man between people with a message, and people looking for information. The media that intermediates for the army is, of course, Hollywood, news, veterans, etc. They are [a part of] pop culture. *But* if you can actually bundle yourself so that you're an *experience*, there is no intermediation.

We had previously been doing TV, radio, print, lots of—legacy approaches without an eye toward the future.

(continued)

(*continued*)

The game industry on the other hand was doing a lot about the future, and now social media and social networking are as well. The Internet just blew up right over the game's time frame.

GBM: So, this was about developing a direct channel with the end user.

CW: Yep, with a target audience who can actually test drive your product. Which . . . nobody can test drive the army. Who is going to buy a car without a test drive, or make a big decision without some kind of trial period? Well, it's a similar situation with the army; there's no test drive.

GBM: What were some of the ideas you had in terms of the design of the game?

CW: We wanted to own everything. Once you make an avatar, a truck, a piece of dirt, or a tree, it's yours forever. And you get to reuse it; you can make it once and sell it as many times as you want. That's what we wanted to do except we aren't trying to make money on the game. So this set the stage for everything we did after that. We had control. We had rights.

GBM: How did you attract the people you ended up using to design the game itself?

CW: We didn't; I think they found *us* once we picked the technology. Creative people are out there making things, making money. We needed to figure out how to grab the tiger by the tail and go for the ride; and we came to realize that the way you do that is to own your finished product and figure out how to access the best technologies. In the end, we hired development firms. They work on specific things for us that we own when they're done. They manage the employees, but the product is managed by the army. So, it's a hybrid situation, and the agenda is ours.

Bringing Players into the Game

In *America's Army*, the people playing the game are immediately aware of themselves as players. They have, after all, agreed to join and download a *game*. However, the parameters for game-play are not always as clear in game-based marketing. A customer may only intend to purchase a widget, not begin a full-fledged battle. Competitiveness researcher Dr. John Houston of Rollins College asserts that highly competitive people create competition even when there is no obvious "game" afoot (for more on this, see chapter seven). But, as the section on passive play showed us, not everyone is equally attuned to the signals of a game's kickoff. So, how *do* designers clearly indicate the start of a game?

Designating a method of enticing players is an obvious step in the development of Funware. In addition to Facebook applications, traceable reward cards or numbers are an effective way to track players' activities and are the model used by most loyalty and FFPs.

Safeway, the fourth-largest supermarket chain in North America, is one such physical goods retailer using a well-known rewards card. In every one of the company's 1,700-plus stores—and in almost every checkout experience that adds up to its $40 billion in revenues—users are exposed to offers for the Safeway Club Card. Discounted items pepper the stores; their reduced prices are available immediately if shoppers will simply enter their phone number or scan their club card at checkout.

Yet despite the strong reward incentive and 30-second sign up, only 1.2 million customers have signed up for the Safeway Club Card program. By comparison, nearly 30 million people visit a Safeway store *each week*. Although the club card take rate seems small at first glance, recent research has shown that only 2.5 percent of consumers account for 80 percent of the average brand-name product's revenue. So, these users are actually among the most important and frequent shoppers at the store.

While consumer groups like CASPIAN (Consumers Against Supermarket Privacy Invasion and Numbering) object to the data collection and use practices of supermarket and drugstore loyalty schemes, over 85 percent of Americans and Brits are members of these programs. Clearly, programs work for the company's simple data-gathering objective. Though there is much more that can be done to convert them into full-fledged Funware programs, supermarket loyalty cards provide streamlined consumer entry mechanisms.

The Future of Fun—The Safeway Club Card

Despite being the fourth-largest grocer in the United States and purveyor of a club card program with 1.2 million members, Safeway is missing great opportunities to build game mechanics into a product that everyone loves: *food*. Some ideas for how Safeway could capitalize on the power of the company's database through Funware include the following:

The Healthy Safeway Club: Designed to encourage healthy and organic eating, leaders in this club could receive badges that label them as "Green," "Greener," and "Greenest." A leaderboard could indicate Safeway's healthiest shoppers and reward players with special recipes, discounts, and even a "healthy dinner on the house."

The Foodie Safeway Club: This club would focus on people who love food and who are interested in taste, texture, and style. These players' goal would be to socialize with other foodies while also maintaining an interest in sharing their knowledge of food with others. Badges should allow players access to better eaters with more knowledge, and the resulting leaderboard should be highly visible.

The Savings Safeway Club: Players in this game would be most concerned with buying and preparing inexpensive meals and should be categorized by family size. Rewards could include tips for savings and social interactions with people with small budgets who are interested in eating well. The community options for sharing savings strategies are almost limitless.

In each case, the different motivations of the various players could be exploited to accomplish the core objective: increased loyalty that's targeted to different styles of "play."

Tracking Behavior

In the context of online Funware tools, virtual currencies and Web cookies are both effective ways to track the behaviors of users—individually or together. If Safeway and other supermarkets took a more holistic Funware approach, they would offer points, levels, and badges to consumers in exchange for their loyalty and the completion of fun challenges. One could easily imagine a daily challenge in a local store that took the form of a scavenger hunt or perhaps a running leaderboard beside the checkout counters that showed the healthiest eaters in the area.

But perhaps even more interesting, Safeway shoppers could be offered an avatar in a parallel virtual world that would be customizable based on points earned in the store. Your virtual character's general health and well-being would be taken from the kinds of foods you ate (and virtual activities, like exercise or travel). This approach would let Safeway mesh its "Ingredients for Life" slogan with an aspiration-driven community experience that would create lasting loyalty and brand passion. By layering this Funware option on top of their highly visible entreaties to *get in the savings game* (discount messaging throughout the stores), loyalty card retailers like Safeway could build greater meaning and connection.

Meaningful Status Displays

One critical component of levels and status is how they're displayed. As discussed earlier, it's important to be able to brag about status achievements without actually bragging. Therefore, successful Funware applications must provide consistent, positive feedback to users about their accomplishments in a social setting.

An easy way to mark users' advancement is to change the appearance of their home page or avatar. Where their pages once were red, achieving the "Super Shopper" rank might turn them gold. Similarly, an environmental badge could be displayed through green branding. If a program issues cards, they too should reflect this change in stature, much as an FFP might. Not only does this present an opportunity to badge players, but in purely virtual worlds, a sink is also created: charge points to players for the issuance of a new card or branded merchandise.

As players ascend to new levels, it is also important to create meaning in their newfound position. As you will read in chapter six, FFPs have developed thoughtful and meaningful levels even though they are fairly standard across companies. While Safeway may not be able to create red carpet lines and waiting rooms with plasma TVs, the company *can* let top customers use special checkout lanes or visit an upgraded virtual gym online—all powered by an intelligent point system and clever level design.

While virtual economies form the foundation for most sophisticated Funware—and overall play is enriched through the experience of levels and badges—much can be said for the use of challenges and games of chance to deepen player interest. Generally speaking, games and challenges can either be won through chance (casino-like play) or skill. Both types of mechanics can have a profound effect on a player's motivation and satisfaction, and both work hand in hand with levels, badges, and points to build powerful customer loyalty.

Key Concepts:

- Point systems let you incentivize many behaviors and fine-tune the value of actions and cost of rewards at will.

- A robust virtual economy—with dynamic earning and redemption opportunities—is a powerful tool in the loyalty game, and designing and managing it is easier than you think.

- Users don't need to redeem virtual points for cash in order to be incentivized by the economy.

- Badges and their conspicuous display are an essential mechanism for conveying and reinforcing user success.

- Levels and status are powerful tools for creating loyalty and driving user behavior.

- *America's Army*, one of the most popular games of all time, has used points, levels, and badges to profoundly increase the market for new recruits.

Prizes and Games
of Chance

The Ansari X PRIZE: The Power of Games
to Change the World

Government-sponsored space travel has lost a lot of technical momentum since the mid-1980s. Other than launching a few minor celebrities and millionaires into low Earth orbit, the world's space agencies have made little advancement. Most people probably remember thinking that by the year 2010, humans would occupy a permanent base on the moon, conduct exploratory trips to Mars, and maybe even experience space tourism, but it seems that without an epic conflict or challenge (such as that offered by President Kennedy in 1961 of "landing a man on the moon . . . and returning him safely to Earth"), there has been no major progress.

Dr. Peter Diamandis, head of the X PRIZE Foundation, thought there was a way to break the world out of its space torpor. He enlisted the help of the Ansari family, successful Iranian-American entrepreneurs and founders of Telecom Technologies and Prodea Systems. They had a simple albeit brilliant premise: if cost-effective space launches were possible, the government would no longer need to serve as intermediary between space and man. And if a competitive market in space launches could be created, then the talents of industry, science, and individuals would be unleashed.

But the world's space programs require trillions of dollars to cultivate, and each launch costs millions of dollars. With NASA and the Russian, European, and Chinese space agencies holding a virtual monopoly on this costly, cumbersome technology, from where would innovation come?

93

Perhaps unsurprisingly, the answer was: *a game*.

The X PRIZE issued a challenge and hundreds stood up to meet it.

On September 29, 2004, the sweat of 27 mostly small tech teams finally paid off. Backed by universities and private funds, these pioneers brought some brilliant and outlandish ideas to fruition. A manned spacecraft named *SpaceShip One* successfully soared into low Earth orbit—and then returned.

The prize, after repeating the experiment on October 4, 2004: a cool $10 million.

Of course, many millions of dollars had been spent to get the team to this point, but the achievement was colossal for both technology and humanity. Interestingly, the X PRIZE game had accomplished something that laissez-faire forces could not. Governments clearly had no competitive mandate, with the space-race era of Kennedy challenging Kruschev long gone. Further, the world's aerospace companies were getting no customer pressure to build space vehicles, and the largest airlines were struggling just to stay afloat in their earthly pursuits. So, in the absence of a forcing factor—from consumers, enterprises, or the government—there was no pressure on the market to design inexpensive space travel.

If the end justifies the means, the Ansari X PRIZE was a resounding success. However, as a game, it did have some substantial design flaws. With its "first-past-the-post" winner philosophy, many other technological advances incremental to the final goal may have been lost. For example, if one of the teams developed a highly efficient engine as part of the process but failed to get into orbit first, it received nothing. And as we already know from examples as diverse as lotteries and massively multiplayer games, having only one prize leaves out a big part of the target player audience. So, beyond its clarity of message, does offering a large prize actually *limit* the ultimate value of a competition? Does offering ever larger rewards hamper Funware's success?

Future X PRIZES

Since 2004, the X PRIZE Foundation has grown and shifted its focus to include endeavors beyond spaceflight based primarily on the notion that games (principally sweepstakes and prizing) can create substantial change. Some of the foundation's challenges include:

- The Archon X PRIZE for Genomics, with $10 million in prizes for teams that successfully and cheaply sequence the human genome.
- The Progressive Automotive X PRIZE, a competition to build the first production-ready 100MPG car.
- The Google Lunar X PRIZE, offering a $20 million purse to the first team to land a rover on the moon that travels 500 meters and transmits high-definition images.

For more information about the X PRIZE Foundation, visit xprize.org.

Can't Buy Me Love: Choosing Prizes

While the $10 million Ansari X PRIZE would be enough to motivate most of us, it did not compel aerospace giants like Boeing and EADS to throw their considerable resources into the ring. At the same time, the objective wasn't quite *small* enough to truly solicit the domain expertise of the world's population in general; that is, there was no way to effectively "crowd source" the required intelligence. Therefore, countless interested scientists, thinkers, and philosophers failed to emerge merely because the game offered nothing for them.

But money has rarely been the motivation behind history's great thinkers. When the goal is the accomplishment of something truly inspirational—be it something as grand as designing a vehicle for space travel or merely motivating a consumer to evangelize a product—it's rarely inspired by money. This is not to say that games are always made *less* effective by the introduction of prizes but rather that prizes often distract marketers, designers and players from the true objective of the game.

One thing that large prizes do exceedingly well, particularly in the context of a long-term Funware project, is to generate media exposure. The X PRIZE Foundation estimates that the Ansari X PRIZE generated six billion media impressions worth over $120 million. Of course, that kind of exposure is difficult to buy—at any price—and should be a consideration in the decision to include large prizes in Funware designs.

Similarly, incrementalism—the advancement of a business objective through a series of small steps rather than big leaps—is frequently driven by money. People will potentially buy one more bottle of soda to get that winning bottle cap or pick up an extra lottery ticket . . . just this once. But to get consumers to go out and tell everyone they know that this is the best soda on earth—to bring them back to buy another soda once the contest is over—is understandably more complex.

Profound invention and abiding loyalty cannot be easily bought with prizes. But you *can* affect behavior for a moment in time, and this can be achieved through games of chance.

Games of Chance

The X PRIZE was a game of skill; players had to be able to build a spaceship, launch it, and bring it back to Earth safely. Conversely, games of chance do not require a player to display a skill in order to win. Most casino games, lotteries, and sweepstakes are clear-cut competitions of random luck in which billions of people regularly take part. In fact, these are the world's easiest, most popular, and most habit-forming games. While we'll discuss lotteries later in this chapter, most games of chance require a consumer to complete a simple action (send in a homemade video, buy a ticket), after which a winner is chosen at random.

From a player's standpoint, the important distinction between a game of chance and one of skill is that the former presses psychological buttons like no other. People become accustomed to a particular stimulus because it gives them a particular reward. And if the reward's payout cycle is variable, then addiction to that particular stimulus tends to rise substantially. This phenomenon is known in psychology as *operant conditioning* and is the principle on which slot machines are based. Other common features of most slot machines are to increase the prize possibility with a larger "bet" and to reinforce winning with massive stimuli such as lights and sounds. Combined, these features are also the reasons why so many people become enslaved to casino slot machines, the world's number one nonchemical addiction.

But games of chance are not inherently evil. When designing a Funware application or using games in a marketing or branding context, including games of chance is an easy way to create excitement and play off the power of operant conditioning among consumers. Even the feedback *language* of slot machines—lights, bells, whistles—is designed to heighten that sense of success and the anticipation that precedes it.

Giving a customer a random slotlike reward—without any warning or obvious tie to his or her current behavior—is something that holistic Funware designs frequently include. A nonspammy pop-up that says "you win" or a periodic opportunity to spin a wheel or scratch off a ticket accomplishes this objective handily.

Of course, rewards make people feel good. If that reward is tied to an activity that a marketer is trying to incentivize, then he or she is likely to get the added benefit of encouraging that behavior more frequently, though there are some concrete legal and ethical challenges that rapidly emerge.

Games of Chance and the Law

Games of chance are often heavily regulated in a way that skill-based games are not. In a weight-lifting competition, for example, there exists a clearly defined skill element. The law doesn't need to dictate how a weight-lifting competition should be scored, nor does it regulate the rules for participation. The guiding principle is that contestants can assess the validity of such contests sufficiently to make an informed judgment about whether to take part. In a game of chance, however, the stakes may become very high very quickly, and the incentive to manipulate them grows exponentially with the size of the pot. The law has therefore evolved to control such games, which conveniently protects government-run lotteries as well.

In order to receive an exemption from antilottery laws, most marketers use sweepstakes as a prizing tool. The principal distinction between a legal sweepstakes and a lottery is that in a sweepstakes, there must not be substantial consideration (investment of time or money) from players. Recognizable phrases such as "no purchase necessary" or "send a self-addressed, stamped envelope to . . ." typically accompany most legal sweepstakes. The definition of consideration is somewhat variable, but the general premise is that if you require players to purchase a product in order to enter the game, you must provide a free method of entry as well.

Despite some regulatory hassles, sweepstakes remain viable tools for marketing and a large industry in their own right. Dozens of companies offer outsourced sweepstakes compliance services, and hundreds of Web sites exist to inform consumers about sweepstakes opportunities. Over time, as companies bring more consumers into a universe replete with increasingly sophisticated Funware and games, rules and complications are likely to increase. For example, if a financial institution began to skirt the line between a casino game and a Funware design—say, by offering random cash rewards at an ATM—users may be negatively affected by increasingly addictive behavior, eventually meriting substantial attention from regulators.

In all fairness, ATM fees are probably as insidious as any game that JPMorgan Chase could concoct. However the objective of prizes and Funware is to create long-standing customer loyalty. Can big prizes bring customers in and keep them coming back?

McDonald's *Monopoly* Game: A Case Study

As discussed in chapter one, the *Monopoly* game at McDonald's is a good example of a long-running, highly effective branded game of chance. During the promotion period, consumers receive game pieces with every purchase at McDonald's. Some tokens provide instant winnings while others are collectible assets similar to those in the eponymous board game. But this version has clear-cut tie-ins to the company's business objectives. For example, a player may order an Extra Value Meal, but if he or she supersizes it, the customer might get an additional game piece or two. Once a player has collected one of the winning sets or receives an instant-win piece, he or she can trade it in for one of several prizes.

The game serves McDonald's well. It generates consumer buzz, creates positive brand reinforcement, and produces valuable media exposure. The number of impressions, magazine articles, and incremental revenue brought into stores during the time of the promotion is meaningful. However, as it stands, the game is really about traditional and potentially broken PR concepts – such as the idea that prizes always drive positive press. This way of thinking can achieve only temporary goals in a socially networked world.

The *real* opportunity that games and Funware provide—long-term customer loyalty—has thus far eluded both the game's designers and the corporation itself. Instead of being a year-round, loyalty-oriented game, McDonald's Monopoly is a short-term promotion that is also becoming less profitable to run over time. A thoughtful, complex, and decisive initiative to encourage McDonald's customers to eat at the chain more often and become evangelists for its positive attributes would clearly do more for the company in the medium term. For a brand like McDonald's—which already takes quite a beating from those concerned about health and safety, obesity, and globalization issues—it's going to take more than a million dollar grand prize and some local radio station coverage to fix what ails it.

Like all prize-based games, the biggest weakness of McDonald's Monopoly game is that once the promotion is no longer running, there is simply no incentive to be at the restaurant. Those customers whose visits to the fast food chain increase during the game's run are bound to return to old habits. But more important, if McDonald's hopes to attract *new* customers through the *Monopoly* game—especially individuals with political and moral objections to its brand—it cannot rely solely on this promotion to motivate these people. For noncustomers without political objections, the game appears fairly involved from a design standpoint, requiring a multivisit commitment in order to play for the largest prizes.

If, for example, we imagine McDonald's *Monopoly* as a year-round competition, we can imagine consumers earning points for any number of activities, including eating at the restaurants, responding to surveys, evangelizing the product, and creating viral videos. Consumers might even choose to play in teams, pooling resources to complete challenges such as "eat at every McDonald's within a 20-minute radius of your home." These activities would allow customers to earn points and elevate their status. McDonald's might even offer badges to customers who propose new menu items (Chef) and those who taste test new products (Sous-Chef). Although this game would be more expensive than *Monopoly* to construct in its first year, long-term value would undoubtedly more than make up for the difference.

The existing game likely brings McDonald's some incremental dining dollars, however the real opportunities exist in converting this game of chance into a program that would run year-round. If marketers could shift their focus from a short-term design that's intended to get return visits from their current clientele to a long-term loyalty program, opportunities to engage consumers and generate positive branding would blossom. And no one has to give away millions of dollars to do it.

The Value of a Prize

Games of chance—when paired with more complex and holistic Funware architectures such as leaderboards, points, and badges—are a highly effective way to enhance or renew brand interest as well as inspire excitement about an ongoing game. Later in the chapter, we will look more deeply at virtual rewards. For now, let's try to understand the value—both intrinsic and perceived—of prizes that are offered.

As mentioned earlier, governments have long regulated lotteries, which allows them to preserve a substantial revenue stream. Consider what effect competition would have on this multitrillion dollar industry. For example, if Mega Millions offers a $200 million prize for $1 per ticket, a competitor might offer the same $200 million prize at a rate of 75 cents per ticket (never mind that the odds of winning—something most people rarely estimate correctly—may be unequal). The probable outcome is that people will continue to play at the same rate; however, those who play lotteries regularly would likely shift money to the "looser" game. It would be a race to the bottom, with lottery companies settling for the thinnest margins necessary to maintain revenue share and consumer interest. Meanwhile, what appears to be a consumer "win" (more lottery options) is eventually eviscerated by gradually lower prize purses and poorer odds.

Of course, in the case of a lottery, the only necessity is the game of chance. The customer's loyalty is "bought" by the weekly prospect of winning a cash prize. If you could legally offer consumers a regular cash payout for purchasing your product—whatever it was—it would probably fly off the shelves (if the success of the state lottery is any indicator). However, awarding regular large lottery jackpots is not legal.

Instead, consider what would happen if a popular dating site such as Match.com or eHarmony.com decided to implement a version of Funware by which a nonmonetary game of chance was incorporated into the fabric of the site's user activity. The concept: "pop-up" matches. While scrolling through a database of potential suitors, prospective mates might randomly find themselves "awarded" with a possible match.

In exchange for extra time on the service or a priority listing, Match.com might encourage users to precommit to going on a truly "blind" date, one that was automatically set up by its algorithms. By nudging the date to occur (and requiring participants to report afterwards in order to earn those reward points), Match.com would accomplish two business objectives:

1. Obtain real, unfiltered data about the efficacy of its search engine that could be used to refine algorithms in a way that isn't possible without having "closed-loop" data; and

2. Encourage users to find mates beyond their obvious points of interest, growing the pool of potential suitors and raising the likelihood that people would find a match (a win condition).

To wit, by merely framing the match's "reveal" in slot machine terms, daters would be more enthusiastic about meeting the other person and taking advantage of the date's opportunity than if results were returned as part of a regular query. In short, making that initial connection would be more fun.

Funware at Play: Slideshare.net

On Slideshare.net, professionals can share lectures and presentations wrapped in basic social networking features. The site tracks the number of times presentations are

(continued)

(*continued*)

viewed, shared, "liked," and commented on. Users' presentations are then featured on the Slideshare homepage or in the "Spotlights" section, the site's version of a leaderboard. If a particular presentation enters the top-ranked group (or even when it's made a favorite)—the creator receives an e-mail notification that is framed as a "win." Since attention and accolades are valuable to most content creators, this social reinforcement is perceived as a genuine prize. The e-mails also have the effect of encouraging authors to reengage with their content and the site—a highly effective "prize" that comes at no cost to Slideshare. The site's leaderboards include the following:

- Hot on Facebook
- Hot on Twitter
- Top Presentations of the Day
- Spotlights
- Most Viewed
- Favorites
- Latest

Long-Term Motivation and Customer Loyalty

The biggest danger to using games of chance in marketing is the tendency to believe that they are sufficient to motivate users over the long term. While a sweepstakes is running, attention and response rates will be extraordinarily high, but once the game ends, so too will its perks.

Sweepstakes tend to be a lazy method by which to incorporate games into marketing. That isn't to say that games of chance are inexpensive or even easy to pull off; in fact, more often than not, the *opposite* is likely to be true. However, the arbitrage of a prize worth 60 cents of every dollar it brings in (as in a lottery) is what marketers continue to trade on. In the typical calculus of a sweepstakes, the prize money, cost of operations, and marketing expenses are added up and compared with the expected benefit, usually sales revenue or PR attention.

In the future, however, large-scale sweepstakes and games of chance will continue to lose traction with consumers in comparison with the long-term rewards offered by better or holistic point architectures. Big prize winnings will continue to be the subject of competitive TV shows. However, it bears mentioning that popular shows involving competition-as-narrative— such as *Project Runway* and *Top Chef*—actually *don't* offer huge prizes to their competitors. The opportunities for exposure and learning—in short, the "soft prizes"—are the true rewards.

We've argued throughout this book that loyalty *must* be the central focus of marketing itself—and the dark side of prizing proves that point. Choosing short-term gains at the expense of long-term benefit robs brands of the consumer mindshare they should be gaining in order to establish loyalty. Worse yet, excessive prizing can encourage users to "game" the system.

Gaming the System

Whenever there is a substantial prize at stake, people will try to game the system. In rough terms, gaming the system occurs when a game's rules are used against itself in order to meet the same objective without undergoing the designated procedure. This is a real risk in all games of chance and many Funware designs. For example, once an unethical player understands that sending a Twitter message about a soft drink to a friend earns him points, he may click the send button—even when he doesn't mean what he says. Thus, users have a perverse incentive to create fake accounts and press the button all day long in order to collect points. In an advanced version of this exploit, users might develop automated "bots" that use software to push buttons hundreds, thousands, or millions of times in an effort to amass points.

Designers therefore find themselves caught in a cycle whereby they're attempting to prevent people from gaming the system but conversely making the game prohibitively complex. Some of the techniques used to thwart such exploits include Captcha (a series of letters or numbers the player must type into a box in order to discourage bot programs) or other balancing methods (e.g., "You can only send one tweet per hour"). Designer and player thus become locked in an endless arms race of increasingly sophisticated gaming attempts and countermeasures. Meanwhile, honest players find themselves frustrated by the hoops they must jump through merely to engage in contests and play. And while cash isn't the only prize people will game the system for, it certainly increases the incentives to do so.

Obviously, good design has to consider the idea that people will attempt exploits. Often, however, by building in more holistic Funware—instead of simply having prize or point or redemption schemes— it becomes substantially easier to control this behavior. One of the better examples of exploit management can be seen in the interplay between badges and flagging, specifically on powerhouse Web site Amazon.com.

Amazon Reviews: Community Policing at Its Finest

Amazon.com's review system is a sophisticated tool that millions of people use to write critiques on the hundreds of thousands of products stocked by the world's largest e-retailer. The review system includes badges for activities that users complete—including reaching the Top 100 reviewers—or for excellence in reviews for a specific product category.

One of the basic design considerations for Amazon.com was that people, in an attempt to game the system, would write simplistic or nonsensical reviews many times just to earn the Top 100 badge, for example. Amazon.com counteracts this tendency by encouraging its users to rate and flag every review. By promoting this behavior and surfacing the badges throughout its ecosystem, the site creates an incentive for others—who've perhaps already been badged —to report their peers' misdeeds. Though Amazon.com could certainly do more work in this sphere, it is among the world's best examples of community policing.

A similar scenario occurs at the airport when people in the premium boarding line check each other's boarding passes while waiting for their turn at the security checkpoint or boarding pass scanner. In a self-policing move, frequent flyers may tell non-frequent flyers, "This may not be the line you're supposed to be in." Or they'll point out, "This is the First Class line." Some will loudly proclaim to a gate agent, "What are the rules to be in this line?" in an effort to shame the person who isn't supposed to be there. We've all been a party to a gaffe, intentional or not, in this arena.

Using Sweepstakes to Fight Gaming

Despite these success stories, self-policing generally remains an insufficient way to keep games from being manipulated. Again, the bigger the reward, the greater the risk of unethical activity. Marketers should be aware that if they do their job right using Funware, consumers *will* eventually attempt to exploit their system.

Sometimes, however, sweepstakes can be used as a method for *reducing* gaming—instead of as an incentive to engage in it. Small, random rewards often encourage users to write bots, whereas single-drawing sweepstakes in which an entry is pulled out of a hat are more difficult to game, especially if the marketer allows a forensic analysis afterwards to ensure compliance. The winner must ultimately be unmasked and contacted, so good database searches can be used to ensure that no duplicate entries are received. On the other hand, if the winner of a sweepstakes is chosen by popular vote, the incentive to "stuff the ballot box" may be too great to pass up.

Although not completely effective, using virtual points instead of cash as a reward may dampen the likelihood of an exploit. If a player knows that you can—at anytime—claw back his or her winnings and the points can't be easily redeemed for real-world goods, you can create a substantial barrier to cheating.

Virtual Points and Prizes

There are a number of benefits besides security to combining sweepstakes/chance games with virtual currency. For example, virtual currency sweepstakes, casino games, lotteries, and other games of chance are largely outside the scope of current regulation. Under such a system, if you can't redeem points easily for cash, you can certainly push the envelope a bit, at least for the time being.

Moreover, building a sweepstakes that trades in virtual currency allows something seemingly insignificant in someone's daily life to be *made* valuable. One need not give away the real house, the real car, or the real jackpot in order to get people excited about a game. As previously demonstrated, the *perceived* value of points can be as great as cash for many users, and the more invested they become in the game environment, the higher the virtual currency's meaning. This goes for badges and levels as well.

Games of chance are easy to bring into a Funware architecture that treats the loyalty puzzle as a whole and delivers prizes as part of the economic system. This approach saves money and reduces gaming risk while reinforcing the overall objective of any Funware initiative: long-term customer loyalty. Moreover, there are hard facts to prove that virtual games with virtual currency and rewards are far "stickier" over time than giant sweepstakes. In the same way that the X PRIZE advanced space travel technology (and arguably, humanity) at 10 times the speed of NASA or the Russian Space Administration's efforts over the past 10 years, the massively multiplayer online role-playing game *World of Warcraft* gets people to play with a longevity to which sweepstakes could never even compare. According to the Daedalus Project, the average *World of Warcraft* player spends 21 hours per week playing – the equivalent investment to that of a part time job or university degree.

A complex game design replete with points, badges, and levels—that also incorporates games of both skill and chance, *World of Warcraft* compels players to invest more time, attention, and money—and may even manage to ruin more marriages—than the McDonald's *Monopoly* game could ever hope to. A game like *World of Warcraft* has created tremendous value, and through game-based marketing, there is no limitation on a brand's ability to derive similar benefit.

While the power of Funware is only now being truly exploited by leading-edge brands, some marketing games are already changing the lives of not just their players—but also anyone who comes into contact with them—for better *and* for worse. Families have been torn apart by these games, their sponsor companies have ceased to be able to exist without them, and consumers eagerly change their behavior to take advantage of the opportunities they present.

These games are played globally, 24 hours a day, and with a competitive edge that rivals that of professional sports. The place is the airport, the games are frequent flyer programs, and the players are all of us, even if you've never joined.

Key Concepts:

- Large prize-based challenges like the Ansari X PRIZE can have a profound "forcing" effect on communities.

- Although prizes generate a lot of PR buzz, they don't deliver lasting loyalty in and of themselves.

- Games of chance are powerful tools that should be used in broader Funware designs, but they suffer from some limitations, both regulatory and user driven.

- Self-policing can manage some of the risk of gaming the system, but that threat is omnipresent. Combining prizing and games of chance with Funware's virtual currency can deliver powerful results.

The Ultimate Funware: Frequent Flyer Programs

U nited Airlines is the other man in our relationship, claimed NYC-based luxury home-goods designer Jason Evege, CEO of Linoto.com. Evege went on to liken himself to a frequent flyer widower, not unlike the millions of *World of Warcraft* widows who claim disaffection at the hands of the popular massively multiplayer online game (MMOG). But instead of losing countless hours to such a game, Evege's partner has been lost to United Airlines' Mileage Plus FFP.

"I thought a *mileage run* was the craziest thing I'd ever heard of," Evege said. "A normal person doesn't fly from New York to Singapore, turn around, and come back the same day just for miles." Although it sounds crazy on the surface, movies such as 2009's hit *Up in the Air*, merely reinforce that Evege's experience is not particularly unusual.

While official statistics do not exist concerning the prevalence of these mileage runs—trips taken for the sole purpose of elevating miles or status—a quick survey of premium members of United's Mileage Plus program reveals that more than 80 percent have taken a purely optional flight or circuitous routing for the express purpose of earning miles or qualifying for a game-based promotion. Then there are those serious members who regularly opt for more expensive or out-of-the-way routings simply to earn miles, status, or rewards on their preferred carrier.

Every year, 54 million people do something for United they wouldn't do for god, country, or love: they spend their money and time, risking their health and relationships in pursuit of miles, a flimsy plastic card, and some status. These people are playing a game. And most of the rewards for which they are playing cost the airline nothing—literally.

Frequent Flyer Programs Take Off

Since American Airlines launched AAdvantage in 1981, the FFP has taken on a life of its own—becoming, in many cases, substantially more profitable than the airline's core business itself.

As cited in chapter one, FFPs have almost universally derived their power from the simple premise of their offering: earn points for every flight you take and then redeem those points for fabulous vacations. The value of these points is determined entirely by the issuing carrier's program team, and as the opportunities for earning have grown to include credit cards, car rentals, and fine dining, so too have the redemption choices mushroomed—and become more challenging.

In tandem with this increasingly sophisticated earning and redemption cycle is the FFP's emphasis on status and badges that provide nonreward benefits for users who reach particular travel milestones. Referred to as Elite status, the accomplishment of these objectives tends to come with various perks, including priority in lines, upgrades, and mileage bonuses. In short, airlines have used the FFP as a tool to motivate users to choose their product over other similar commodity choices—the classic example of a highly functional loyalty program.

What Business Are Airlines In?

But how can an airline—whose ostensible objective is to move people and cargo from point A to point B—evolve into the purveyor of a virtual economy (think Supreme Court, bank, and general store rolled into one)? The critical lesson of changing business priorities applies to myriad industries and any brand, company, or venture that is subject to commoditization.

Before the deregulation of airlines began in earnest in 1978, the world's carriers were luxury service providers. They delivered the highest quality of service using the most modern equipment. Pre-1980s airlines were also pioneers in advanced technology, speculatively buying new modern planes (Concorde) and investing in unproven technologies (large-scale computer networks) to compete on service. There might only be one or two airlines on a given route, and a government regulator set their prices. Therefore, the differentiating factors tended to be oriented toward service and technology.

Once the airlines were deregulated, all of these golden perks disappeared—and the airlines' profits with them. From 1990 to 2006 alone, U.S. airlines lost $22 billion, and since 1978, more than 160 different airlines have disappeared from the skies. But in the early 1980s, when differentiating on service was no longer an option, American Airlines decided to begin an experiment that would radically alter its fortunes. The originial AAdvantage of 1981, which bears little logistical similarity to today's program with 60 million–plus members, offered simple rewards for flying and some personalized recognition. Early frequent flyers who achieved 10,000, 20,000, or—then, shockingly—100,000 miles were often rewarded with personalized letters thanking them for their business and numerous in-person benefits.

As time went on, other airlines followed suit, and status levels were added; at-airport benefits began to roll out, and a much wider range of earning and redemption options came into being. Whereas the airlines themselves were engaged in cut-throat competition in their core business—reducing service quality and trying to preserve pricing power—offerings became increasingly rich and varied in the frequent flyer world, though the ability to redeem points in general would become increasingly challenging.

Set against the backdrop of price-based competition and mounting losses across the board, the breathtaking revenue opportunity in FFPs has been ever more attractive. But most important, from a consumer standpoint, the FFP is really the only differentiator of substance among today's largely undifferentiated airline deals. Except for having a bad personal experience with one airline or another, most consumers can't distinguish among the various airline offerings, and they consider all airlines equally distasteful from a service and comfort standpoint. As proof, the airline industry continues to score abysmally on various product satisfaction rankings, ranking at the bottom of major industries in Forbes' annual survey of customer satisfaction. So, how do you sell a commodity product to a consumer that requires substantial investment but seems thoroughly undifferentiated?

By making it into a game, of course—one that is highly addictive, attuned to providing its players with psychological rewards at every turn and that taps into their most basic competitive and status-driven instincts. FFPs are the greatest example of a successful game-based business model.

A Brief History of Frequent Flyer Programs

1981—American American Airlines introduces the first FFP. A few days later, United Airlines introduces its FFP. Delta and Trans World Airlines launch their respective FFPs.

1983—Holiday Inn and Marriott launch their rewards programs.

1985—Diners Club launches the first credit card rewards program.

1987—After longstanding resistance, Hilton launches a rewards program. The first major car rental program is launched at National Car Rental.

2002—Credit card use overtakes flying as the principal way to earn miles.

2006— The total number of worldwide FFP members reaches 180 million.

Designing the Frequent Flyer Massively Multiplayer Online Game

As with massively multiplayer online games—like the previously discussed *World of Warcraft*—FFPs make use of certain key design components. Much like the MMOGs they resemble, FFPs combine all of the critical game mechanics into a unified, comprehensible whole. Once they reach a particular size and intensity, they acquire their own points and levels, designers, support teams, etc.

In the context of Funware design, the FFP example is the most powerful model that can be patterned; its comprehensiveness is an inescapable strength and weakness at the outset. On the one hand, by considering the many aspects of a holistic Funware design (points, levels, badges, leaderboards challenges, rewards), FFPs provide unlimited customization options and true flexibility. In effect, United Airlines can use its FFP to sell airline seats, meals, even mortgages.

Conversely, this complexity can be a turnoff to new players and those with expectations based on other FFP experiences. For example, Starwood Hotels Preferred Guest program lets users convert their points into airline miles to be used with almost every major carrier in the world. United Mileage Plus, by contrast, allows almost no transfers. This difference in expectations can create substantial conflict.

When building Funware, a designer need not start with a complex game design on Day 1. However, he or she must consider the business' objectives as well as how it will come together in the long term. While many of these Funware and game mechanics have been discussed in previous chapters, the focus here is on understanding them in the context of an FFP design.

United Mileage Plus

United is the world's third-largest airline and the oldest commercial air transport company in continuous operation in the United States. Although well known for its customer service blunders, contentious employee relations, and frequent trips to bankruptcy protection, the airline has also been a significant innovator. United has managed to win—some would say clutch dearly for life— the affections of its business customers through the power of its Mileage Plus Program.

Currently the second-largest FFP and anecdotally the most active, Mileage Plus is a large company in its own right. Although revenues are not reported separately, the division is likely to be worth substantially more than the airline operation itself.

Like most FFPs, Mileage Plus offers various status tiers (Premier, Premier Executive, 1K, Global Service) that reflect miles flown per year and revenue generated for the company. Mileage earned can be redeemed through product and travel partners (such as magazines, hotels, and rental cars) as well as on flights on United itself or one of its airline partners.

The program is regarded as an innovator, being among the first to offer a defined tier for revenue contribution (versus simply miles flown), status tiers above one million flown miles, team-based mileage challenges and competitions, and worldwide, multipartner games. In a given year, Mileage Plus offers as many as 50 different promotions and challenges, giving its members an unprecedented opportunity to earn points and status.

The Power of Points

FFP Funware begins with a comprehensive point system that assigns both earning and redemption values to a virtual currency that cannot be converted easily into real cash. The lack of convertibility essentially helps designers and marketers maintain control over the virtual economy and their ability to manipulate its levers. Unlike a simple point system, however, an FFP's virtual currency is typically earned and redeemed across a much wider range of activities because once it's sufficiently subscribed to by users, it gains an extant value of its own, much like a real currency.

Earnings opportunities in FFPs are often extraordinarily varied; consumers are offered the opportunity to earn points in many different ways that provide incentives for different behaviors. These can include the obvious—flying—as well as many other behaviors. Once the point scheme is deployed, it's possible to fine-tune it to match particular business objectives or promotions at will. Further, once a game has successfully alerted its users to the existence of a point system, it becomes substantially easier to get the attention of its users. This ability to cut through the clutter is one of the principal reasons that FFPs are able to attract hundreds of partners to their reward schemes. When United Mileage Plus sends you a letter or email, you are more likely to open it than a similar, unsolicited mailing from Chase.

The flexibility of point systems to influence behavior is the reason they are so prevalent in sophisticated games and Funware. Let's take a look at a powerful use of points to motivate: asymmetric earning. The following is the table of point earnings for various tickets on United for a 1,000-mile flight:

Fare Type	Elite Qualifying Miles Earned
First Class	1,500
Business Class	1,500
Full-Fare Economy Class	1,500
Discount Economy Class	1,000

The most noticeable item on this chart is that First, Business, and Full-Fare Economy Classes offer identical *Premium* point bonuses. Instead of providing progressive bonuses for each class of service as might be expected, there is effectively only one level of incentive: upgrade from Discount Economy Class to any other class.

Beyond that, this point scheme tells us something much more interesting and reflective of consumer behavior: 95 percent of air travelers book Discount Economy Class. Passengers who book Business and First Class tickets usually book Business and First Class—incentives or not. So, the focus of this point structure is to push the *marginal* Economy Class ticket buyer into becoming a full-fare ticket buyer. The bonus is relatively substantial as well because the incremental revenue for the carrier is 100 percent profit.

Making Money on Virtual Currency—the Frequent Flyer Way

If it's clear to you that Funware mechanics can benefit your marketing initiatives, you have probably considered the implementation of a point system or the expansion of an existing one. But beyond a simple lever—or nudge—for encouraging user behavior, a robust virtual economy can become a substantial income stream in its own right.

Once users are wedded to your virtual currency, they will become interested in investing their cash—as well as their time—to purchase your points when they don't have the energy, time, or desire to earn them the "hard" way. The most obvious example is to allow users to purchase certain amounts of virtual currency directly with cash. A "top up," if you will, allows users to quickly obtain a reward they seek without having to go through the usual steps (flying). Airlines and other MMOG designers have turned this tension between time and money to their advantage, raking in billions in point purchase fees for a commodity that can be obtained, nominally, for "free."

The other revenue stream for virtual currency is to sell it to third parties that offer it as an incentive in their businesses. Some of the largest frequent flyer program schemes, such as United's Mileage Plus or American AAdvantage, earn billions of dollars each year selling points at wholesale prices to credit card companies, car rental agencies, and incentive marketers. These points are then redeemed for no cost or otherwise perishable redemptions, providing an extraordinarily high-margin opportunity for the issuers.

Getting There without Points

If a business wanted to accomplish the same fare upgrade objective without a point system, conveying the same information in campaign format would be hopelessly complex. It would also require an influential salesperson at the point-of-sale moment encouraging the upsell. Much like the option to supersize fast food orders for incremental payments, conveying an upgrade value proposition without a point system requires frontline team training, an articulate representative (or well-crafted user interface), and sufficient time in that harried moment to explain the benefits of choosing the upgrade. While both approaches are valid and often used together, the longer term orientation of the point scheme makes this process easier and more durable.

Simply put: if a user is invested in accruing points, he or she is more likely to be knowledgeable about your incentive offers and more receptive to receiving those offers in the first place. Moreover, the technical cost of creating, implementing, and managing a point system, as pointed out in earlier chapters, may ultimately be much less than the alternative over the medium term. Once the infrastructure is in place, it's relatively easy to keep track of every actionable item, and this gives the FFP one of its core cost advantages over standalone promotions.

Real-World Redemptions: Do They Matter?

As any frequent flyer can tell you, the flipside of point accrual—redemption—is a perpetual cat-and-mouse game that pits the Funware designer against the customer base as an economic unit. The objective is to make the points as desirable as possible while minimizing the cost of the redemptions that users try to obtain.

However, one critical lesson that incorporates learning from FFPs and the MMOG world, which this book intends to hammer home, is the fact that effective loyalty programs built on Funware do not necessarily *require* real-world redemptions. Even if your customer base is used to trading in stamps/points or loyalty for physical goods (with marginal costs), the increasing traction of virtual worlds provides even the most traditional brands with the opportunity to switch redemptions to cost-free options.

The Solution Is Virtual Goods

The 2009 market for virtual goods is estimated to be approximately $5.5 billion worldwide, with tremendous double- and triple-digit growth expected in all major markets. These small online items range from virtual gifts (including cards, cakes, and animals to customizations in the virtual world (room or avatar décor); to power-ups that can be used in the context of traditional games. As the prevalence of virtual goods increases, the options for offering these low-to-no-cost items increase. Whether it's purchasing redeemable points in existing large-scale virtual worlds (at a fraction of the cost of frequent flyer points) or creating an environment of your own where virtual goods redemption is meaningful, the economic value here is substantial.

In the FFP model, established goals are more often married to real-world status. However, users are usually willing to exchange their points for *opportunities* for more points. They will even join other loyalty programs as long as those programs agree to convert their points to miles simply in order for them to get more points. For example, over the years, hotel programs have offered rewards across the "friendly skies" and beyond by partnering with airlines, rental car agencies, and other travel industry ambassadors.

Research indicates that in many cases, convincing internal stakeholders to support a Funware program (specifically as a replacement for established sweepstakes) becomes easier when there is a connection to real-world product rewards. It's critical in these circumstances to structure the redemption in such a way that encourages users to choose the least costly options while still offering them a satisfying use of their time and effort.

In this way, the point system continues to offer a tremendous advantage over other, more program-oriented marketing options. Funware designers can use its flexibility to dynamically adjust the redemption rates to suit then-current business objectives. For example, let's assume that your core product is soft drinks, and you've designed a virtual-world Funware loyalty program that allows redemptions for free beverages. FFP-style Funware can be used to dampen or raise demand in particular products. Consumers may be introduced to less popular soft drinks by lowering the points necessary to try them for free. Real-world and virtual parties can be encouraged, where a particular soft drink is used in food preparation and cocktails. The top rated or best attended parties win points. Airlines are masters at deploying their programs to match inventory/sales conditions—and you can use their techniques with ease.

But Does Redemption Matter?

While it may sound Machiavellian, the frequent flyer example suggests that once users have established a perceived value of miles or points, their need for immediate redemption—and the positive feedback that goes along with it—tends to decline. For example, in 2007, there were nearly 10 trillion unredeemed miles sitting in the world's frequent flyer member accounts. Considering that amounts to approximately 50,000 miles per user and the average person only earns 11,000 miles per year, the "savings" rate in the FFP world is astonishing: FFP members *bank* an average of five times their annual earnings. By comparison, the average American saved just over 5 percent of his or her annual cash earnings in 2009.

This steep gap in self-control belies a critical fact: every unredeemed Funware point or mile represents revenue generated by the airlines along the way. Although the points may eventually be redeemed—and are often accounted for as a liability in financial statements—the general spoilage rate of FFPs is quite high. Whether the points expire or members simply forget to redeem them, this behavior helps justify the investment in FFPs.

Still, there is no question that consumers value redemption opportunities. In fact, most FFP promotions lead with a statement about the benefits of redemption in order to encourage users to sign up. However, the low rate of redemption clearly illustrates that consumers care about more than just free flights and hotel rooms; they care about playing the game itself. While this can present a challenge for traditional marketing strategies that assume consumers only want rewards, the upside is tremendous. FFP point systems reduce the marginal cost of providing rewards and allow their designers to finely manipulate user behavior in sophisticated ways. In short, they are the perfect solution.

But if hundreds of millions of players worldwide don't care *that* much about rewards and redemptions, what does motivate them to engage in FFPs with such gusto?

Status, of course.

> The number of unredeemed frequent flyer miles in the world is a staggering 10 trillion. Did you know that it would take over 23 years at normal redemption rates to reduce that to zero—assuming that consumers didn't earn a single additional mile?

Levels and Badges in FFPs

It's clear in the world around us that status is a powerful motivator. Having perceived high status is itself a reward in both the physical and virtual worlds. Studies by prominent researchers such as Ball and Eckel in their 2001 "Status in Markets" suggest that high-status individuals are happier, better adjusted and seem to achieve greater outcomes in most business situations, including better jobs and improved posture in negotiation.

But while elaborate rituals have evolved for the display of status appropriate to our social norms, most people struggle with the challenge of how to share pride in their achievements without seeming boastful or crass. It's one thing to bring people in to see trophies atop the living room mantle; it's another entirely to attend a dinner party with a track and field medal around your neck.

As Lampel and Bhalla successfully argue in their research titled "The Role of Status Seeking in Online Communities," the difference in status behaviors between online and offline communities is eroding. Little evidence suggests that motivation varies based on the milieu.

Airports and airplanes are a nexus of extraordinary displays of status—both desired by the players and encouraged by the Funware architects themselves. From First Class lines to premium waiting areas, airports offer dozens of literal examples of the dividing lines between individuals of differing statuses. Velvet rope and VIP lounges abound on the ground, while a curtain, seat comfort, and even special toilets delineate the classes in the air. In short, airports and airplanes provide great "cover" for boasting. Through excellent design, similar opportunities can be created in any industry.

Throwing Your Weight Around

In discussions with many front-line airport employees, one topic comes up over and over again: entitled passengers. From a brief interview with a gate agent: "Not a day goes by that someone doesn't say 'I'm a Premier Executive, and you need to get me on that flight.'"

Of course, such brazen (and poor) attitudes are generally frowned upon by other passengers and the employees who find themselves in the line of fire. But where does this sense of entitlement come from? Does the individual-cum-player always use that tone and affect when trying to get things done in the world outside the airport? Or has the airline itself *encouraged* this behavior through the design of its level architecture?

The answer, most likely, is the latter. As players rise through the ranks of their FFP of choice, they become accustomed to being able to use their status for increasingly greater rewards and flexibility. Whether they are granted boarding or standby priority or merely recognized for their loyalty through a direct communication ("thanks for flying with us so frequently"), high-status airline flyers are encouraged to think of themselves as special. And, in general, they are.

United's Mileage Plus Program has nearly 54 million members. Of these, an extraordinarily small group (1.5 percent) has achieved Elite status with the airline:

Status Level	Miles Flown per Year to Achieve Status	Total Number (2005)
Premier	25,000	535,000
Premier Executive	50,000	239,000
1K	100,000	46,000
Global Services	(revenue based)	18,000
Total Premium		**838,000 (1.5%)**

But this small group of premium flyers has a disproportionate effect on the airline's revenue. Estimates suggest that as much as 40 percent of airline revenues are generated by the top 5 percent of customers and that over half of all business travelers—

already the top spenders—chose their airline based on the FFP they were principally engaged with. It therefore seems valuable to cater to these customers through a status-oriented system, especially considering the lack of overall redemption activity (and its marginal cost). In almost every business, it would be useful to surface and focus on the top customers. In fact, this is the very reason American Airlines launched AAdvantage way back in 1981.

Benefits of Status

Since, as we noted previously in our discussion of VIP lounges/areas, status is substantially less rewarding unless others are aware of it, airlines have become masters at giving consumers a demonstrable status opportunity in the real world. In analyzing the airport operations of United at San Francisco International Airport, it becomes obvious that the airline seeks to create clear opportunities for status conveyance. Here are principal places where status is clearly displayed:

- A Premier lobby for Elite customers
- Priority check-in desks and automated kiosks
- Priority security checkpoint
- Extra-priority security line "jump" for Global Services Members
- Red carpet boarding lane for Elite members
- Boarding announcements done by status order

This list does not even include the priority handling given to Elite customers—including Elite member–specific telephone operators—that exists beyond the general purview. In short, it's impossible to transit through a modern airport without being confronted by the profusion of ways that higher-status passengers are having a better time than you.

And this system serves a critical purpose: it both reinforces the positive associations that Elite customers have with their program and acts as a form of direct advertising for the program itself. Because nonstatus passengers can see the benefits with their own eyes, they are encouraged to consider playing the game "harder" if they want to gain those benefits in the future.

Such obvious win-wins need not come at a great cost to the brand/product either. Most of the core benefits of status can be conferred with minor incremental expenditure. Consider the principal benefits of the various levels of the mileage plus program:

Tier	Miles Flown Per Year to Achieve Status	Benefits (incremental)
Premier	25,000	Priority boarding, waitlist, check-in Economy Plus access Star Alliance Silver status No checked bag fees Complimentary full-fare upgrades 25 percent mileage bonus
Premier Executive	50,000	All Premier benefits plus exit row preassignment International Lounge access Star Alliance Gold status Priority baggage 100 percent mileage bonus

Tier	Miles Flown Per Year to Achieve Status	Benefits (incremental)
1K	100,000	All Premier Executive benefits plus systemwide upgrades No award fees

Waitlists and standby are generally handled in status order, so 1Ks receive substantial advantages over Premier Executives and so on.

A quick analysis of the chart reveals two very interesting things. First, most of the benefits accorded users have little-to-no direct cost. The biggest perks (like upgrades) are capacity controlled, so the airline only offers them when it doesn't expect to sell a seat for cash. Most of the other advantages—like checked bag fees—are purely opportu-nity-cost driven and weren't revenue sources until very recently.

Second, the greatest benefit "jump" occurs when a member first becomes a Premier member. That is to say, the incremental benefits provided at each level of status are nominally smaller than that received at the first Elite level. Of course, this reflects both economic reality and extraordinarily good game design thinking. While the first tier of achievement is generally hardest for a new player, and the economic effect for the designer is greatest in moving users from nonstatus to status, the rewards should provide the greatest "pop" immediately. As users progress within the game, their expectations for recognition reset such that incremental benefits seem substantial. And while the 1K upgrade certificate benefits may seem exciting on the surface, a regular Premier member wouldn't fly enough in a year to make those certificates worthwhile. To wit, such benefits are very expensive for the airline, so they are held for the company's best customers.

Artificial Scarcity

One of the most interesting things about the "nickel and diming" of air customers is that most of these new fees don't apply to the company's Elite members—a very smart decision that both creates loyalty ("I don't want to pay those fees again") and appears to offer a benefit, even though it's a purely artificial construct. The FFP designer *created* scarcity and then provided a benefit around it. What could be cheaper than that? Consider ways that your business can create artificial scarcity using Funware design.

The Level Error of FFPs

While FFPs tend to be among the best-designed Funware in the world, there are a number of lessons from online game design that FFP designers could incorporate to improve their performance.

- *Offer an opportunity to level up much sooner than at 25,000 flown miles.* This would go a long way toward promoting more engagement with the game and the airline's products. In most MMOGs and single-player games, users are offered a chance to level up very early or a badge reward to encourage them to keep playing past the first few levels. Increasingly, this reward is made available literally after levels one or two, although FFPs tend to set the first bar extremely high. Perhaps flyers could receive a positively reinforcing level up or badge on their first flight (free drinks come to mind). Consider including early reinforcement in your Funware design as well.

- *Offer simpler, smaller rewards for smaller loyalty.* If the average person only flies 10,000 miles per year, it would be worthwhile to offer some kind of status reward to match his or her likely flight patterns. Casual game designers routinely endeavor to make their games easy to pick up but hard to master. FFPs could simplify early rewards and create a tier for the average flyer without taking anything away from truly frequent guests.

- *Casino-Style Rewards.* Reward flyers with random prizes such as upgrades or bonus miles to create short-cycle reinforcement of their motivation to fly. This can be easily done since the airline knows when someone has boarded and could even be delivered to passengers via text message right after their boarding pass is scanned.

Going Above and Beyond: The Boss Level

As we've seen, levels and status play an extraordinarily significant role in the success of a Funware design. Users respond well to status incentives, and their achievements—just like leveling up in a game—should be treated with much pomp and circumstance. When used judiciously and with care, level/status elements can benefit Funware design in all areas, from finance to philanthropy.

But what happens when your Funware program has been hugely successful—as with Mileage Plus' first 25 years in business—and your players begin to beat the system?

In the 1980s and 1990s, most FFPs acknowledged the evolution of their games by introducing a "million mile" status. Individuals who flew over a million miles—an incomprehensible distance for most folks at the time—received lifetime status benefits and special acknowledgement. By comparison, in the 1960s, similar benefits were bestowed on American Airlines customers who flew 100,000 miles. So while it took 40 years for the top level to jump by a factor of 10, it took less than 10 years for it to double again.

By the mid 2000s, thousands of United's customers had reached the million mile status and received their lifetime Premier Executive status. There was nothing else for them to do—no additional levels or benefits to the game (short of reaching for 1K each year). And since it takes the average player over 10 years to reach such a goal, there was a certain amount of fatigue.

The drop off was substantial. While no figures are publicly available, anecdotal evidence suggests that as many as half of all motivated flyers who reach a million miles then focus their flying on other carriers to gain lifetime status across multiple alliances. In effect, these players have beaten the "boss level" and have then become bored with the game.

In response, the designers at Mileage Plus created, in game lingo, an "expansion pack." At the end of 2007, in a nod to its best and most aggressive players, the company officially rolled out its previously informal two million–and three million–mile status tiers. In keeping with the preceding design philosophy, these levels offer incremental rather than breakthrough benefits.

While it's not essential for the average Funware designer to consider on Day 1 what happens when users play past the expected level design, it *is* essential for them to build a status and level system that allows players to keep playing. In other words, don't give away all possible benefits at the top published level. Reserve some intellectual and programmatic space to expand offerings to emerging superstars.

But while status and levels are great tools for encouraging long-term, aligned behavior among players, consumers also need short-term goals that provide psychological and economic rewards. That is, while a player is slogging it out in seat 96K at the back of the plane in order to get to the Premier Executive level, he or she could probably use a minigame for distraction. Enter the challenge.

Challenges and Contests

The intrinsic availability of a virtual economy and status/level designs makes challenges and contests in the FFP Funware design a logical and cost-effective part of a customer loyalty strategy. Principally, the status tiers of an FFP tend to be medium- and long-term achievements for users; months may elapse between no status and the first level, and the same pattern may occur for subsequent levels. Moreover, after a number of years and high levels of achievement, players may become desensitized to the overall excitement of this Funware offering and begin looking for distractions. This creates the perfect environment for challenges.

Throughout the year, FFPs provide their members a wide range of promotions and offers in the form of challenges. Differentiated from typical contests or straight product promotions, FFP challenges invite users to increase the time they spend and their level of engagement with the product in exchange for virtual rewards. Further, some challenges include a social component asking players to form teams and alliances—simultaneously deepening the bonds of loyalty for their brand.

Because the virtual currency has value, these challenges can be executed at a fraction of the marketing and fulfillment costs of a traditional contest. Further, they exist outside the legal constraints governing cash sweepstakes, and they reinforce the basic economic meaning of the Funware itself. In short, FFP Funware actually makes challenges and contests more meaningful for everyone concerned.

And FFP challenges are not limited to action-reaction or sweepstakes entry models at all. In fact, they can be designed to engage users across a wide range of activities and fine-tuned to accomplish business objectives.

> While games and game mechanics offer better long-term user retention rates than any other form of engagement, anyone can lose interest after playing something for five to seven years. Just ask married couples!

United's Team Challenge

In 2008, United launched a novel challenge that was so effective and impactful that it even received a coveted Freddie Award. Mileage Plus members were allowed to form teams and compete to win a share of 50 million miles and upgrades that were being offered as part of the promotion. The teams were ranked on a leaderboard based on the net *increase* in miles flown in 2008 over 2007. The top 50 winning teams each received a million miles and upgrades to divide among themselves.

The challenge generated tremendous attention online. Thousands of flyers participated, forming teams and keeping track of theirs and their peers' performances. By incorporating both a social aspect (choose teams) and a direct business objective (increase miles flown), designers had come up with a contest that was a surefire winner. Of course, the necessary components needed to be in place: a large community of potential players, a point system to track the program, and a simple messaging platform to which consumers' ears and minds were thoroughly open.

It would be difficult to imagine this kind of campaign working as well without the underlying FFP mechanics. And while it doesn't effectively meet the test of making it easy for nonplayers to play, the design does encourage each team to include both seasoned experts and newbies since the mileage delta is the measured behavior. Plus, the buzz that the competition generated was certain to draw the curiosity of nonplayers.

Though most FFP challenges need not be this complex, another benefit of conceptualizing loyalty programs through a Funware/FFP lens is the option to produce targeted challenges and contests that are designed around the behaviors of individual users. Once they have opted in to your passive Funware design, you can offer programmatic challenges that encourage certain activities.

For example, a consumer with a monthly purchase habit might receive a challenge to buy a product twice a month over the next three months in order to win some virtual points. Conversely, users who already purchase three of that product a month may be invited to double their purchases in the subsequent month. Both challenges accomplish the same net financial objective but scale the offer appropriately to existing user behavior. Over time, marketers can even determine which challenges are most appealing to which users and deliver those that matter most. Some users might prefer upgrades, others additional points.

This kind of personalization is only possible and economically viable through the foundations inherent in an FFP: points, status/levels, and challenges that have already been established.

Making It Work for You

Despite the considerable economic effect of FFPs on the aviation industry, there are relatively few thoughtful and all-encompassing approaches to customer loyalty beyond the travel business. As illustrated throughout this book, a comprehensive approach to connecting with consumers is likely to produce optimal results. While direct shortcuts to sweepstakes or simple leaderboards may seem appealing at first, the medium-term investment in a cradle-to-grave Funware system that resembles FFPs is the ideal solution for loyalty-centric thinking.

However, leveraging the FFP to create true customer loyalty requires a small but substantial shift in thinking. Is your company in the business of making widgets or building lasting relationships with its consumers? A marketing strategy that focuses principally on driving sales—with loyalty as an adjunct—reflects the reality of most commoditizable businesses. FFPs accomplish *both* at an impressive rate. We can all learn from their examples and use their power to learn more about our most valuable assets: customers.

Key Concepts:

- Frequent flyer "games" are among the most successful and popular loyalty programs.

- When challenges and a complex series of badges, levels, and points (miles) are incorporated into games, depth and intrigue are added.

- Mileage runs are a not-uncommon means by which players will go out of their way to get more points, and similar behaviors may be generated in other industries.

- FFP games are flexible in terms of rewarding players. Prizes can therefore be customized.

- Points in FFPs are often used to encourage incremental elevations in expenditure.

- Points take on greater real-world value when coupled with other loyalty programs to increase redemption options.

- The virtual goods market is growing rapidly from a $5.5 billion level in 2009.

- Consumers who beat the system or who level out should be given new and improved opportunities.

Know Thy Player

I t's impossible to sell weight loss systems with an obese spokesperson.

This conventional wisdom has guided the health industry for the majority of its existence in the United States. Brands like Jane Fonda, Bowflex, and Bally Total Fitness have used athletic spokespeople whose muscular physiques and smiling faces seem to scream "You want to be me!" at the top of their lungs.

But a quick survey of today's health and fitness landscape will show more overweight and older spokespeople than ever before. Famous actors—many of them in their 50s—who have struggled with their weight and health headline some of the biggest brands in weight loss. Entire swaths of television airtime are devoted to reality weight loss programs in which stars and average people alike compete to lose weight and get healthy.

And in the process, the weight loss and health industry's revenues have skyrocketed. Yes, Americans are now more likely to care about their physical health more than ever before, but the industry has also learned a critical lesson about how to market in an age of game design and Funware: it's no longer enough to know just your customers' *purchase* motivations. You need to know what drives them to *invest, engage,* and *succeed.* The connection between successful weight loss and game-play should be obvious after the preceding section on passive games, and it's a fact not lost on health marketers. Would you rather be a plump, smiling, and actualized Valerie Bertinelli trying to shed a few pounds or a muscular 4 percent bodyfat Bowflex model?

The answer is, unsurprisingly, less about who you are and more about how you want to play the game.

Bartle's Player Types

Over 20 years ago, a professor and forerunner in the development of the massively multiplayer online games industry developed a well-established body of research that can help us produce a simple player typology. In establishing four basic player types, Richard Bartle's research looked at the *motivations* that drive people to play.

The four general player types are represented by the following motivations: Achievement, Socializing, Exploration, and Killing. While each type generally prefers a different style of game-play, they are not mutually exclusive. These four player motivations can be applied to our understanding of daily life as readily as they can be seen in the context of a game. People often respond to one of them more than another, or they may find that they are better represented by a mix of several. By studying their responses to various daily tasks, individuals might see themselves as any of the following:

- *Achievers* relishing the fact that they finished mowing their lawn before the football game (bonus points for completing the task before their neighbors).
- *Socializers* attending a religious service more for the social interactions than for the service itself.
- *Explorers* walking or biking around town, generally enjoying the travel as much as the destination.
- *Killers* doing anything to win an account at work, even if it means tarnishing the reputation of the competition (or their peers).

By understanding these types of players, marketers are better able to channel people into the appropriate challenges and play patterns that map to their interests in a more meaningful way.

However, whereas Bartle stopped short of asserting that Killers might exhibit their behavior outside a multiplayer game (his theory does not articulate his typology in terms of personality), Funware theory makes no such distinction. If someone prefers to "kill" in the context of a game, he or she is also likely to "kill" when faced with a competitive but passive game. And this means that understanding a consumer's play motivation can be as crucial in a game-centric world as knowing his or her age or income. In short, how and why we play is the new demography.

Achievers (♦)

Principally driven by a desire to get points, achieve goals, and hit their mark, Achievers—also known as "diamonds" (as in the suit in a deck of cards)—will typically go to great lengths to acquire points and prestige. For this player, winning may even be less important than playing well. These players prefer games full of bonuses and extras and enjoy acknowledgment for the thoroughness of their game-play. They tend to favor games that appreciate and reward them for completing tasks. Most important, they like winnable games that have an end point.

Another important aspect of the Achiever mindset is the social component. Achievers do not care about winning in a vacuum: they require an audience to appreciate their accomplishments. In this regard, social networks and leaderboards are imperative for satisfying play.

While it may not be obvious, building Funware that only caters to Achievers will generally fail. When Achievers play principally against other Achievers, they are unlikely to get the amount of praise they desire. For that, they must seek out a different player type entirely: the Socializer.

Socializers (♥)

Socializers ("hearts") play games in order to connect with other players. This type of player's desire for social interaction cannot be underestimated. Socializers are less likely to play a game in order to show off their skills than to build meaningful communal interactions. Often they derive greater satisfaction from helping a better, more established player gain points, status, or rewards than from seeking out prizes on their own. Their instinct is less competitive and more cooperative. While collaboration and competition are not mutually exclusive, it's nonetheless instructive to consider them as weak correlates.

Socializers typically establish alliances quickly and take part readily in nearly any type of group play opportunity. However, they must be allowed to observe others' play as much as they partake. This player type is often of great value: after all, their friend lists tend to be lengthy and their allies many.

Explorers (♠)

Explorers are diggers, like the spades card suit for which they are nicknamed. Games and Funware with a set pace tend to be less appealing for these players as they are far more interested in mapping out their environment. The richer the virtual world for this player, the better!

An Explorer is far more apt to prize random puzzles, side stories, and the environment of the game above opportunities to win points or badges toward the culmination of a meta-game. Explorers, however, do not object to games with a limited storyline or objective as they are the players who are most likely to set their own rules and challenges. For example, they are apt to set internal achievement objectives or to define an alternative process for completing the game in its entirety.

In a social gaming situation, explorers enjoy nothing more than to be able to share the detailed and sometimes unusual information they have uncovered about the game or its narrative. Long games that require repetitive behaviors will ultimately bore this keen player type. By acknowledging this player, Funware architects give themselves an opportunity to add depth and richness to their games. Random challenges and puzzles are vital. For the Explorer, the game is all about the journey, never the destination.

Killers (♣)

Killers ("clubs") like to win. As their name suggests, these players are motivated by the joy they experience as they "hurt" other players (in the context of the game, of course.) Killers enjoy competition and prefer social game environments to games where they play a computer or themselves (they rarely enjoy solitaire). Satisfaction is greatest when the enemy can be named.

That is not to say that Killers won't play alone, but simulated win/loss scenarios are essential for their satisfaction. Further, they require many opportunities to win, enjoying status, competition, and an unfair fight—as long as the scales are weighted in their favor.

In a social game, there are those Killers who genuinely enjoy the thrill of killing weak opponents, in some cases repeatedly. Then, in a sudden switch, this same player may derive pleasure from swooping in and saving the day. They like to be good and give other players reasons to be very afraid. Killers don't need love in social games so much as they require respect and power.

This player type relishes win/lose games far above games where winning is the norm. The more chances for Killers to win, the better.

The Naïve Player

Bartle didn't identify the Naïve player, but then again, he wasn't specifically considering Funware and game-based marketing when he developed his player typology. The Naïve player is, simply put, playing the game accidentally. These players may type in a frequent flyer number every time they fly but never so much as add up their points. They may have a rewards card from their bank, but they don't know anything about the game in play.

The Naïve players from chapter two—those who engage in gamelike behaviors while waiting in line for coffee or getting on the subway—certainly exhibit traits from straight out of Bartle's handbook. However, until they become aware that a game is afoot, their Bartlian type is unlikely to emerge.

Funware designers must look at the means available to them to attract Naïve players' attention. Obviously, the best way to accomplish this is to clearly call out the existence of the game that is being played. As described in previous chapters, leaderboards, point systems, and obvious status indicators are great ways to accomplish this. If, on the other hand, a choice is made by the marketer to ignore or dampen down the fact that a game is in play, only the most competitive players are likely to engage, while the Naïve player will continue to trundle along, unaware and uninterested.

The quality of the game suffers when Naïve players get in its way. Just as when a slow and oblivious driver disrupts the flow of traffic on a highway, the Naïve player risks disruption of others' play if he or she is truly unaware of the game.

Since originally identifying the four player motivations, Richard Bartle has deepened his player theory. For each player type, subdivisions have been added:

- Friend
- Griefer
- Hacker
- Networker
- Opportunist
- Planner
- Politician
- Scientist

For more on Bartle's player motivations, consider reading his seminal work, *Designing Virtual Worlds*, available at books.google.com.

Competitiveness: The Most Important Motivation?

Rollins College psychology professor Dr. John Houston has dedicated much of his professional life to the study of competitiveness. He defines competitiveness as, "The desire to win in interpersonal situations." Houston's research has found that competitiveness remains stable over time; he calls it a "state" rather than a "trait" or "characteristic."

The most common archetype for competitiveness concedes that one person encounters an external opportunity to beat another person, and once an opponent is beaten, a "winner" emerges. Interestingly, however, Houston found that those with a high need for achievement instigate competition whether or not there is an obvious competitor. This desire to win is sparked by perception as often as it is by overt gameplay and is equally affected by external cues or internal motivations.

However, Houston also found that one thing is true for everyone regardless of where we fall on the competitiveness spectrum: once two or more people know that there is a competition in play, all parties tend to compete. If neither party knows that a competition is active, the competitive person remains as likely to compete while the noncompetitive person probably won't compete.

Houston also points out that lower competitiveness scores do not necessarily equal high levels of *cooperativeness*. He does indicate that though cooperation is less likely for a competitive person, it's not necessarily a given with less competitive people, and some people seem to dislike competition entirely. However, if a prize is appealing enough to a noncompetitive person—or even an individual who isn't interested in any type of contest-based environment—that person can overcome his or her tendency to avoid these challenges.

"Competitive people," Houston explains, "have a very low threshold for when they will jump into a competition and are likely already *seeking* out ways to compete." Conversely, people who prefer to steer clear of competition may not see it as something worth *pursuing* unless there is some high potential pay off.

Competitive participants are fundamentally important to any Funware design, and their actions and motivations should not be taken lightly. By manufacturing competition whether or not designers want them to, these players can easily alienate others and find themselves exhausting their predefined challenges well before the Funware's expiration date. But when competitive players cease to be engaged, efforts are likely to lose momentum and credibility. Conversely, creating an experience that caters too explicitly to the highly competitive is sure to make others feel like failures. Care and game-balancing are the watchwords for these crucial players.

The following is an excerpt of an interview between the authors of *Game-Based Marketing* (**GBM**) and Dr. John Houston (**JH**). The interview is available in its entirety at Funwareblog.com.

GBM: Have you observed competitive people fabricating competition where there is none?

JH: Actually, that's how I started investigating competitiveness. When I was doing my dissertation, I [looked] at personal and group goals. I was manipulating a lab test [with two outcomes that could take place] once the group reached a certain level of performance. In one, the entire group would be rewarded, and in another, only the best

(continued)

(*continued*)

performer would be. What I found to my surprise and annoyance as I went through my data analysis was that even when I was creating the cooperative situation where everyone would be rewarded—as long as the group reached a certain set of goals—there were a certain set of individuals competing or trying harder to make sure that they were the *top* performers.

GBM: Do competitive people tend to win more?

JH: I've been trying to track down what behaviors are connected with competitiveness. I have looked at things like career choice; competitive people are drawn [to] situations that enable them to engage in competition. For something as extreme as professional sports, for example, world-ranked tennis players turn out to be *really* competitive people with no exception. I think that people who aren't competitive just find that environment too adverse and find something else to do.

GBM: Does a person's competitiveness level affect all spheres of their life?

JH: As a personality trait, competitiveness should cross different social domains. There may be stronger associations with competition based on personal histories and individual experiences. College sports players [for example] do not see themselves as competitive in other domains; they just see themselves [this way] in sports or certain types of games. But as a personality trait, it [typically] generalizes across domains.

GBM: How do noncompetitive people tend to respond to competitive people when they merge in a social or game context?

JH: [We found] in the *Prisoner's Dilemma* game [a game theory exercise where players must choose to cooperate or compete in a "vacuum"] that when a situation clearly becomes competitive, everyone acts [accordingly], so we weren't really able to detect differences. We found that when one side tries to deescalate or provide some conciliatory behavior, competitive people were much slower to respond. Moreover, in clearly competitive situations, we weren't able to predict people's competitiveness scores. Everyone reacted in a competitive way.

GBM: In terms of competitiveness, how would you divide the population?

JH: There are some gender differences. Males tend to be more competitive than females. That tends to be true across different cultures. But there is a more or less normal distribution.

Closing the Gender Gap

A 2005 study conducted by Comscore exposed that the average video gamer is 41 years old. Even more surprising than the shift away from the image of a pimply-faced Xbox player was the research that found that more than half of these 41-year-old game-players are female. The study went on to reveal that people most frequently played games if they had previous play experience or in response to a word-of-mouth recommendation. Anyone who is already playing games will continue to do so, and their interest in those games is expanding.

Some products are decidedly focused on specific genders. For example, one cosmetics brand has developed an online game whereby consumers can upload a picture of their face and then "apply" different products to it to see how they would look on them. The game lacks any competitive quotient and assumes women would be largely uninterested in competitive play (despite evidence to the contrary). Yet there are an endless number of ways in which this game could be deepened and enriched. For example, virtual pageants using peer judges could markedly improve the game. By including points, leaderboards, and badges, players could become "consultants" and then "experts" from whom other players could get information about which products would go best with their skin tone and what to wear to what event.

Nike+: Early Adopter Advantage

Another Funware design that has been getting a lot of attention is Nike+. Because the game is focused on health and fitness, it has an appeal that spans both genders. Similarly, since its goal is to increase Nike's consumer base (after all, a person who is seriously involved in his or her fitness routine will need an increasing number of fitness accessories), the company is inclined to reach out to as many demographics as possible.

Nike+ works with devices that are built into Nike footwear or outboard peripherals equipped to measure how fast a person runs, how hard he or she hits the ground, and how far the runner goes. Data fed to an iPhone or iPod then feeds the information to the Web. The heart of the Nike+ ecosystem is made up of personal and public leaderboards that indicate performance. Since its launch, more than 1.2 million runners have collectively tracked 130 million miles—and burned 13 billion calories. Obviously, Nike+ is the most popular fitness Funware ever developed.

Whereas Wii Fit is a game with fitness objectives, Nike+ is a fitness tool set that uses games to encourage people to become more physically fit. As such, it is liable to have a profound effect on its players. Once they are invested in the Nike+ game, they can begin to compare their physical activity with that of their friends. Mutually supportive virtual exercise groups can form—without their members ever having to meet up for a run. Friends can work out with friends in different states who have different interests or even different work schedules.

Nike's initiative is a great example of how Funware's early adopter companies are gaining substantial competitive advantages over those who come later. By integrating basic Funware components (leaderboards and points, challenges, and eventually badges), Nike is substantially raising the switching costs for changing footwear and accessories. In the past, when your Nike Air Max shoes wore out, you could simply buy a pair of Adidas with no incremental cost beyond the effort of trying them on (something you'd be inclined to do, regardless). Now that your socially networked fitness data is integrated with the kind of shoes you buy, changing from Nike to Adidas has an emotional cost. Purchase a different brand of shoes, and you risk losing historical information and important social connections. After becoming an active part of the Nike+ experience, everything else will just look like sneakers.

But what if Nike+ wasn't constrained by the need to sell the shoes and gear that was the main goal of the parent corporation? What if fitness Funware is Nike's real purpose? We contend that Nike is itself at a critical crossroads in understanding how it defines itself as a company. For more on this discussion, see chapter ten.

Fahrvergnügen's Failure

In 1989 German car company Volkswagen began a marketing campaign using the slogan "Fahrvergnügen," or "driving pleasure." The intent was to brand a lifestyle out of car ownership. With every new Volkswagen sold, people were given, along with the keys, a lifestyle guidebook. New Volkswagen owners felt like they were being inducted into an important social and unmistakably cool group. Driving meant freedom, and Volkswagens meant happiness.

Unfortunately, the campaign's promise was as easily tossed aside as the guidebook. Volkswagen could have been where Apple is today—the leading lifestyle brand for urban, educated people worldwide. But what happened? What did a person truly get from being in the club? Frankly, nothing. Volkswagen offered no virtual or real-life rewards, points, challenges, or badges as part of the Fahrvergnügen campaign. Had the company chosen to do so, perhaps its customers would have developed the kind of loyalty the program's designers originally envisioned. Something as simple as earning area maps for fabulous road trips or tips for achieving better mileage as well as real-world prizes like free tanks of gas, free checkups, and free road trip vacations would have made a huge difference. What if Volkswagen hadn't just *told* people they were in an Elite club but actually *created* a kind of Elite club into which the company put some of those lifestyle promises?

While Fahrvergnügen was a success in raising awareness of the Volkswagen brand, which subsequently sold many hundreds of thousands of vehicles, its lasting effect has been minimal—a sure sign that continued loyalty and a Volkswagen lifestyle did not emerge. Perhaps Volkswagen marketers expected that maintaining a long-term loyalty program would be far less simple than writing a guidebook and running an ad campaign.

However, creating loyalty does not need to be complicated. When a person buys a car, his or her brand investment is substantial; every time the person drives, people see his or her choice. But even in the example of car owners, there tend to be markedly different motivations that drive loyalty—and again, the opportunity to use Funware as a basis to create loyalty is obvious.

Breaking down the company's consumer base, there are Volkswagen owners who are Achievers—those who constantly seek the best gas mileage or perfect deal on a used car. There are Killers—those who would like to be able to show off the power of their vehicle at the expense of others. There are Socializers—folks looking for an opportunity to simply join the community of Volkswagen owners. And there are the Explorers—a group perfectly suited for car ownership and brand connection.

Motor vehicles are ideal products that can be used to exploit the power of Funware and push "players'" various motivational buttons. Because of a vehicle's tendency to create a strong emotional attachment, its ability to create memories and expressive brand identities, and the substantial cash investment required to procure one, it should be a trivial matter for automakers to leverage these factors to form a durable community. Yet, with the exception of certain specialty car owner groups—and those are largely grassroots organizations—this hasn't happened.

Fahrvergnügen, indeed.

The Wrap-Up

From VW owners to professional tennis players, consumers have common sets of wants, needs, and motivations. While marketers have historically considered these psychographic (and related demographic) features in relation to *buying* habits, it is clear that in a game-centric world, we will need to consider these motivations in light of *playing* habits.

Richard Bartle's seminal work on player motivations has shed just such a light. By dividing MMOG players into categories of Achievers, Socializers, Explorers, and Killers, Bartle has given us a simple taxonomy that helps us more readily understand how and why people play. While this analysis benefits from the addition of correlates—the Naïve player and an understanding of competitiveness—it is nonetheless fundamental to our quest to perfect the development of customer loyalty.

While we use Funware design methodologies to make every experience more like the successful MMOGs of the online world, we must also be aware of the fundamental shifts in demography occurring all around us. This game-centric future is being led not only by 40-plus-year-old women, who are the single biggest growth market for games, but also by

Generation G, the most dynamic and potentially misunderstood generation in 30 years.

Through their constant exposure to games and game mechanics, today's tweens are setting the stage for a revolution in everything from banking to books, ATMs to IRAs. Generation G's future is bright—but will you understand these consumers?

Key Concepts:

- Bartle's player motivation typology is one way to consider targeting future players.
- Achievers, Socializers, Explorers, and Killers are four player types.
- Naïve players do not know they are engaging in a game.
- Even noncompetitive people will compete in competitive situations.
- Nearly half of all online game-players are female.
- Brands that implement games early will be at a distinct advantage over latecomers.

The Future of Gamers: Generation G

A Generation Gap

Not since the time of the Vietnam War has such a profound generation gap existed in contemporary society. However, our intergenerational communication challenges these days don't pivot on a global political conflict. Rather, if you were born after 1998, you are part of a generation that is more technologically savvy, socially networked, and competitively oriented than any other in history.

If you are one of the approximately 20 million Americans born between the years 1998 and 2000, you are part of Generation G, the first large demographic group whose principal form of entertainment is games. And if you're a marketer seeking to communicate with these potential consumers—or someday will be—this point needs to be extra clear: they will change *everything*.

What Makes Generation G Special?

Generation G has grown up thoroughly wired to the Internet; as of 2003, nearly 50 percent of Americans were on broadband. Members of Generation G are also leading the social networking charge: more than 7 million of them regularly play on the hybrid game/social-networking site Webkinz. Once you add the rest of the tween-oriented social sites, it's not a stretch to predict 100 percent penetration for social networking in this demographic. Just as e-mail accounts went from being nearly nonexistent in the early 1990s to the principal method of communication on college campuses within 10 years, social networking will likely achieve a similar importance in much less time.

It also goes without saying that G'ers are also expected to become mobile savvy. With the increasing penetration of iPod Touch, OLPC/Netbook PCs, and network-attached handheld devices like the Nintendo DS, this group is set as well to be the first truly *mobile, social* generation.

But while all these technological advances are substantial—and their effects shouldn't be minimized—these platforms (Internet, social networking, and mobile phones) have been targeted to an older and more affluent audience, which has readily adopted the technology as its own. In fact, even though smart phones (such as the iPhone, BlackBerry and Android) and social networks like Facebook have rapidly become the dominant social memes of the moment, kids under the age of 13 are almost nonexistent in those spheres. And while women over 55 are the fastest-growing demographic on Facebook itself, the site doesn't even publish data on the number of users below the age of 13.

It isn't that kids of this age aren't actively online, socially networking, or using mobile devices; it's that they're engaging in these activities principally through *games*. Just as they are most impressionable, entering puberty, and discovering the power of social connections, games have become the principal metaphor they use to interact in the world around them. Whether carrying their Nintendo DSi, meeting new friends on Webkinz/Club Penguin, or anxiously awaiting the latest networked toy from Smith & Tinker, Generation G has its priorities—and game-play easily tops that list.

The Trends

In 2005, a Dutch marketing agency uncovered evidence that more than 60 percent of children under the age of 18 play video games on a daily basis. Furthermore, despite the popularity of gaming consoles such as the Playstation and Wii, this study also concluded that 65 percent of these games are being played longer on computers than any other platform. By late 2007—after only two short years—a new study saw these numbers rise. In fact, one-third of *all American children* consistently increase their rate of game-play from one year to the next. The 2007 study indicated that by age 10, most children with a history of game-play have already added both mobile and handheld games to their repertoire of computer and console experience. No longer tethered to living room devices, games are now portable and consistently available. You might even say that ubiquitous gaming is now a reality. And the trend is deepening.

To further understand Generation G's play habits: about half are considered light users, those who play games fewer than 5 hours per week. The rest of the population is divided into medium, heavy, and super users, with the last category spending upwards of *16 hours per week* playing games. In fact, many of these super users are inclined to migrate to portable systems between the ages of 6 and 8. These children tend to increase their game-play by 3 hours per week—or 75 percent—over these years. The gaming industry recognizes that this is the age at which children are most likely to set patterns of play that will stay with them as they age. The rate of play is seen to plateau between the ages of 12 and 17, reaching an average of about 10 hours of play per week.

Computer Play Is Good for You

The increase in total time spent playing games and the "stickiness" of computer-based games offer great news for marketers looking to include games as a core strategy. Although teaming up with popular brands and developers on platforms such as the Wii, Xbox, and Playstation isn't impossible, creating and implementing games and Funware on the Web is substantially more cost effective. PC and online games also offer added flexibility: changes and updates can be made on the fly, and marketers are not tied to the one-shot launch effort of a $5 to $10 million AAA game title.

Smith & Tinker

Jordan Weisman is the CEO and cofounder of Smith & Tinker, a company that designs toys that marry online games with offline socializing. As Weisman explained, "Kids [ages] 8–12 have grown up living and breathing on the Web and as such, have moved to online gaming as their principal form of entertainment very early in life." The result, he said, is a group of people with little interest or patience for the offline toys and games that have satisfied every previous generation.

Weisman, a well-known game design, author and serial entrepreneur also noted that games with a social component tend to interest kids far more than solo game-play. In his estimation the missing component from many online gaming experiences is quite simply, *the rest of your life.* In other words, Weisman believes there are—and should be—ways to combine online play with everyday activities. More importantly, the children who use his products *expect them to.*

"Eventually," Weisman stated, "these super computers we carry in our pockets are going to aid us in interacting with each other rather than cocoon us from each other."

Weisman knows of what he speaks. In 2001, along with Steven Spielberg, he developed one of the most influential early alternative reality games called *The Beast*, which ran for 12 weeks to promote the film *A.I.: Artificial Intelligence.* The game used real-world tools such as cell phones and in-person discussions with actors playing the characters. In *The Beast*, players took on the roles they were given and incorporated only those characteristics in real-world contexts.

Weisman's products continue to reflect this trend, and their popularity is an easy indicator that he is right on target.

The authors sat down with Smith & Tinker's CEO Jordan Weisman (**JW**) and Senior Vice President of Marketing Charles Merrin (**CM**) to get their take on Generation G.

GBM: What have you learned so far about the players of your games and their expectations for what is "fun"?

JW: Ultimately, if you go back to the beginning of time, games have always been about socialization. They are a medium for communication; a common ground. The

(*continued*)

(*continued*)

same is true of sports. They're the nonliquor equivalent to get conversation going. Ultimately, every great game builds that context around itself. The same is ultimately true [of] working with younger kids. It's the context of the community and your accomplishments within that community. Your ability to gain some recognition from the community in which you are emotionally invested is the greatest motivator for people at all ages.

GBM: How do you react when people use the term "social games"?

JW: With rare exception, this concept is straight out of the "Department of Redundancy Department " to me.

GBM: When do you think kids start to care about the badges-and-levels construct?

JW: Probably in the womb. I guess I've never seen a kid that doesn't want to be recognized.

CM: Even kids that start playing as soon as they can begin [to do so]—which these days is ages two, three, and four—[they're] already online, always wanting to show off: "Hey, look what I did!" It's a sense of achievement for them . . . a sense of pride. Or a sense of whatever drives a three year old at that point. I've seen it from Day 1.

GBM: Do you find ways in your design to make it easy for kids to show their parents and their peers? Or is your focus toward peer expression?

JW: I think it's principally peer; but I do think that being able to present progress to parents is an important component. Kids look to [their] parents for recognition; they want that pat on the back. I think it's sad, but I don't think too many parents place value in what their kids accomplish in games and thus don't see it as something they should give [credit] for. But the kid had to actually *work* to accomplish it; and they want that [acknowledgment].

GBM: Some people claim that the connected toy market (toys that work both on and offline) threatens the future of traditional toys, but how do these toys threaten established social networking?

JW: In the sense that opening a new ice cream parlor can take business from an old ice cream parlor. Any entertainment product is in competition with all other entertainment products, and social networking sites are ultimately entertainment products. I think we would hope that kids are spending a lot of time on our site, and that probably means that if they are getting their socialization with more of a structure around it—because of a gaming component here—they may visit social networking sites less.

CM: Ultimately, social networking is a means to an end; not the end itself. If you think about it, many of the [stronger social networking] sites [just encourage and allow] people [to make connections] and chat with [other people utilizing the site].

GBM: Has there been anything in your audience's behavior that has truly surprised you in the extensive testing you've done on products before they've been made public?

CM: One thing I found sort of unique—and that [differs quite a bit] from what I expected—is [that the kids seemed] to be extremely open to new ideas. I expected kids to come in with an opinion of what a toy should be, what it was, and what it wasn't. Here was something they'd never seen before, and to see their eyes click, "Oh!

(continued)

(*continued*)

I can do that with that and that?" To really grasp a completely new idea; to see how natural it seemed to them.

JW: One [interesting thing] was that we started with this assumption that the handheld devices needed to be wireless because to us older folks, wireless is pretty cool. [However], we were having real trouble finding an affordable wireless solution that could have the bandwidth of communications we needed. So, we'd come up with this concept of physical connection where the device is magnetically connected and the screens become one large virtual screen so your character jumps to another guy's screen. We tested that against wireless with the kids, and it turns out [that the desire for wireless is] just one of those generational things. The kids we were talking to grew up with wireless, so there's nothing magical about [it] to them.

CM: In fact, it's almost the opposite.

JW: Exactly. This physical connection was [pretty special to them], and the way that they jumped from screen to screen really got them excited. So, it's honestly one of those generational things; the modern miracle to us is common as salt to them.

GBM: Five or 10 years in the future, what are today's kids going to be like? What enthralls them as far as game content is concerned? How do you keep those kids engaged after they've tried something as engaging as this?

JW: I think one of the things about the [audience like] the ones we're dealing with—and up to their 20s, maybe 30s—[is that they have] no concept of what the previous divisions of older types of media used to be. What is a TV show? What is a radio? What is a movie? What is a game? What is a book? The fact that they are totally separate industries with [completely distinct] economic structures is irrelevant to them; they don't understand any of those divisions. And they don't understand why the story they want to be involved in isn't ubiquitous across all these mediums and through all these devices that they carry with them every day for a very seamless experience.

The Gulf Is Real

It's easy when looking at the following table to validate the reality that the pace of technological innovation is accelerating and that Americans' appetite for new technologies, particularly those related to games, seems to be rising as well. The fact is that Playstation sales would not have been possible without the widespread existence of household televisions. Interestingly—on an inflation-adjusted basis— the first Playstation 2 cost a mere fraction of the price of the first TV.

Time to Reach 50 Million Households/Subscribers in the U.S.

Television: 25 years (1938–63)[1]
Broadband Internet: 19 years (1986–2005)[2]
Mobile Telephony: 14 years (1983–97)[3]
Playstation 2: 8 years (2000–2008)[4]

It's worth noting that Playstation 2 is the best-selling game console of all time and that we're comparing a single device against an entire industry. But this only lends more credence to the thesis that games are more attractive than other platforms.

---

1. www.tvhistory.tv/Annual_TV_Households_50-78.JPG.

2. www.websiteoptimization.com/bw/0404.

3. www.p2pays.org/ref/19/18713/cpch2.pdf.

4. www.blog.us.playstation.com/2009/01/ps2-sells-over-50-million-units-in-north-america-breaks-console-sales-record.

However, the biggest and arguably most significant difference between Zeniths, RCAs, and Playstations is the person who is buying them. The first 2 were introduced targeting older demographics. In fact, their high price tags meant they could not be purchased by anyone who wasn't wealthy by the standards of the day, or at the very least, who wasn't a working professional. In contrast, Playstation 2 was priced as an affordable, kid-friendly product that could easily be purchased with a few months worth of paper route money or as a reasonably priced birthday present for the average middle-class family. Once a product lifecycle targets children, it readily becomes both highly lucrative and extraordinarily influential.

Games and Gender

Playing games is a far less male-centric pastime than previously thought. While boys do tend to play at video game consoles more readily than girls, girls are equally drawn to game-play when they encounter it on cell phones and PCs. Much of the drop-off in female game-play after age eight is generally thought to be the fault of marketing. Marketers are already taking notice and discovering the possibilities in the realm of technology for girls. A steady upswing in interest marks the success of these trends.

One way in which using games to market to children of both genders is especially apparent is when the game relates to television programming and movies. Nearly all modern children's television shows include some option for online game-play. For example, the Web site for *Hannah Montana*, a show with a decidedly female or younger child bias, features a fashion game whereby the player can dress up the primary character on the show. The Cartoon Network has managed to target both genders at once by creating a single game that incorporates characters from both the popular series *Dexter's Lab* about a boy scientist and *The Powerpuff Girls* about a team of girl superheroes.

The Effect of Games: Tetris, Team Building, and Tug of War

While it's difficult to empirically determine the effects of game-play on young children, some research has been conducted that has both quantified the effects of game-play and observed the emergence of key social trends that may be related to gaming. From this related research, we can add to our hypotheses about Generation G.

In 1992, University of California at Irvine neuroscientist Richard Haier conducted one of the earliest studies on the effects of video games on the brain. His study ultimately deduced that video games seem to make brains work more efficiently. By studying the brain scans of players learning the popular puzzle game Tetris, Haier discovered that as their skill levels increased, their brains required less glucose.

In a recent study also led by Haier that was published in the summer of 2009, the team unraveled research from a group of nongamers against another group of Tetris players. These studies again proved that the efficiency of brain function markedly improved as the players' skills improved.

But while few of us doubt the effect of games as tools to hone certain kinds of skills (consider flight simulations), what about the broader effects of games on behavior, character, and expectation? In this realm, the available research is murkier but nonetheless intriguing.

Bing Gordon, venture capitalist and former chief creative officer of Electronic Arts, famously quipped that many "kids are learning to read for the first time playing video games." Similarly, former Xerox chief scientist John Seely Brown has written on the topic of *World of Warcraft*'s positive effect on leadership skills in the workplace. Rollins College professor John Houston additionally noted that even non-competitive people become engaged with a challenge once it is made obvious. He also pointed out that college students appear to be exhibiting more competitiveness over time—even so far as to dampen some of their collaborative cultural heritage in favor of gaming the system (our words, not his).

So, while there are no definitive data on the specific result that game-play has had or will have on Generation G's consumption of marketing and advertising messages, the related scientific evidence suggests that games are having a profound effect on even the most basic of personality traits. It isn't a great leap to believe that these changes will intensify and fundamentally alter the perceptions of today's tweens.

The Character of a Generation of Gamers

Pre-G generations were clearly influenced by similar, if less intense, trends. Videogames have been around since the 1970s, and modern social networking was really popularized by those born in the mid-1980s. As anyone born in the past 100 years can comfortably assert, the pace of technological change has always been intense. However, it appears to have increased even more rapidly in recent years.

The most germane difference that we must understand and appreciate is the importance of *fun*. Consider a set of activities you might choose for an hour of downtime:

1. Watch TV.
2. Read a book.
3. Do your taxes.
4. Play your favorite game with your friends.

If you are one of the few individuals who are excellent at understanding long-term costs and benefits, your first question is likely to be: How many days until April 15th, and how big is my refund? However, if it is any day other than April 14th, chances are that you are far less likely to file your 1040 than to challenge your mother to an online Scrabble game. Despite the clear incentive *not* to do so (and get your refund faster), a quarter of Americans will still wait until the *last possible day* to file their taxes.

Procrastination itself is sometimes the product of simply having better choices. If, as in the example above, you're not subject to an immediate penalty for not filing your taxes, odds are that you—like a majority of people—will choose the activity that is more rewarding now over the one that is more rewarding (or less punitive) in the future. Put another way: pleasure today is substantially more valuable than pain tomorrow. So if you grow up on a steady diet of games—expecting all the powerful reinforcement, flashing lights, and social connection offered in today's best interactive entertainment— and you have 60 minutes of penalty-free downtime, what activity will you choose?

Now, what if some of the activities that were once perfunctory are suddenly fun? What if reading a book had all the same psychological rewards of playing a game? What if cleaning the house reinforced all the positive attributes of self that you get from spending hours on *Gaia Online?* What if doing your taxes made you giggle with delight? What if you could win at *anything?*

That's what we can assume members of Generation G will count on when they become a viable consumer demographic. They will expect it of their jobs, their social lives, and their entertainment—and they will certainly expect it of their advertising.

 ## The Future of Funware

Why Can't Taxes Be Fun?

Past efforts to inject some fun into tax season have, predictably, fallen flat. Not that the accountancy industry is generally known for its sense of humor, but some of the attempts, like H&R Block's *The Deductor* game, have been particularly poor.

And yet, tax returns seem like the perfect opportunity to deploy Funware.

Some suggestions for tax preparation companies and Web sites alike include the following:

- Leaderboards for lowest effective tax rates, highest deduction increases, and so on
- Challenges for tax preparation professionals to find the most eligible deductions, games that they can play with their clients

- Virtual point options for tax refunds that allow taxpayers to convert their refunds into other products—virtual and physical—at a discount and as an alternative to receiving cash.

Conclusion: Successfully Marketing to Generation G

The central challenge of marketing to members of Generation G is principally to meet their expectations for fun, challenge, and sociability. Because of their exposure to games, they have come to expect this potent mix of benefits in every aspect of their lives. Additionally, Generation G—and most of today's other savvy consumers—have a virtually unlimited range of possible choices for how they will spend their spare time. The net result will be a volatile cocktail wherein traditional marketing messages and two-dimensional advertising don't stand a chance. Consumers will simply choose not to engage with such marketing messages. They will—in the language of DVRs—skip the commercials whenever they can.

Just as today's subway riders are rarely looking at the ads above their heads and are instead content to be buried in their iPhones and iPods playing quick casual games, so too will tomorrow's consumer—Generation G—be oblivious to traditional messaging. Whether it's virtual worlds, augmented reality, or just choosing the bank with a gamelike ATM, members of Generation G will vote with their avatars for everything to be more fun.

However, by understanding this dynamic and the drive to play, socialize, and win that underlies G's game-centric lifestyles, you can successfully market to this emerging and influential group of buyers. By bringing the power of games and

Funware to marketing and branding, you can create experiences that are at once quotidian and challenging, inspirational without pandering. It's this intersection of game mechanics like challenges, rewards, levels, and badges that—when blended with your underlying product or message—will be the most interesting. For those companies that "get it," the opportunities will be tremendous.

The Future's So Bright

As games become more central to the average American family, researchers predict the following inevitable trends:

Number of households with next-generation video game consoles by 2012 (worldwide)	190 million
Percentage of those consoles connected to the Internet	80%
Percentage of households that will use those consoles at least one time per week	75%
Percentage increase in the number of households playing wireless games from 2002 to 2006	20%
Percentage of parents who see video games as being a positive part of their children's lives	63%

Rating of the top four best-selling video games of 2009	"E for Everyone"
Fastest-growing entertainment software since 2007	Family Entertainment (110% from 2006 to 2007 alone)
Gender breakdown: Who plays more games?	Women 40% Men 60%
Percentage of American teenagers between the ages of 12 and 17 found to play games in a study conducted from November 2007 to February 2008	97%

Key Concepts:

- Generation G is the most technologically savvy, competitive, and socially networked.
- Among all demographics, game-play is most prevalent on personal computers.
- Half the demographic of G'ers are light users, but the rest range from medium to super users.
- Price points for new technologies are far lower, indicating a younger target audience.
- Games are no longer solely targeting boys, and more girls are playing.
- Kids who grow up on games are going to expect gamelike experiences in all aspects of their lives.

Motivating Sales with Funware: Getting Employees into the Game

G ordon Ramsay is among the world's best-known celebrity chefs. One of his television shows, *Kitchen Nightmares*, helps struggling restaurants reorganize and restructure. One episode featured Campania, a family restaurant in Fair Lawn, New Jersey. While the close-knit staff had no problem getting along at work, pushing menu items was not their forte. As a result, the restaurant suffered from excessive spoilage, losing thousands of dollars from rotten food on a weekly basis. At the same time, it often sold out of the more popular menu items, leaving customers in the lurch. Despite having a loyal client base, the restaurant's problems had begun to make a serious dent in its bottom line.

In order to fix the problem and save Campania, Chef Ramsay did something revolutionary for the restaurant business: he implemented Funware.

At stake: $100. The challenge: Campania waitstaff must sell one of every item on the menu in a single dinner service. The result: No oversold items and no leftovers.

Front Line and Top of Mind

Although his was a simple solution, Chef Ramsay understood that games—including challenges and rewards—can be powerful drivers for frontline sales teams. If, as in the restaurant business, your company's success depends on the interplay between marketing and sales, this is a critical piece of the game-based marketing puzzle. It's where direct-to-consumer marketing leaves off, where customers are often confronted directly by frontline employees, and where communication and product knowledge directly affect the outcome.

While there are many ways to motivate sales teams, this chapter focuses on using Funware from the vantage point of the marketer. No matter how closely aligned the marketing and sales teams may be, the actions of those who are on the front lines of customer service have a direct effect on all areas of business. The sales team's mindshare and loyalty are critical, and creating synergy with Funware in the marketing sphere is a valuable objective.

Of course, Funware is not a new concept in employee motivation. Employees of the Week can win everything from a prime parking spot to a picture on the wall. Chances are that each one of us knows someone who has won some kind of on-the-job award. To wit, sales motivation strategists agree that ongoing competition helps stimulate sales and incentivizes positive job site etiquette. Simultaneously, simple leaderboard games can grow tedious through repetition and tend to lose their meaning over time.

Funware has the power to change employee motivation in a way that was impossible previously in business. The corporate opportunities to create team play between consumers and sales teams are endless. More important, the marketer's ability to invigorate sales and keep consumers engaged becomes a matter of tweaking existing game mechanics and adding new and exciting challenges. Once a game is in play, the well-crafted step of adding points, badges, and levels is guaranteed to strengthen the loyalty of both consumers and the frontline employees with whom they come into contact on a regular basis. Not only will they sell every meal on the menu, they will continue to sell meals for as long as the game is in play.

Frozen Treats, Fully Staffed

"The hardest thing about running a retail business is hiring and retaining the right employees. Though we've been extraordinarily lucky to have some great long-term staff, it's a real challenge." —*Patama Gur, CEO & Founder, Fraiche Yogurt*

Fraiche is a wildly popular yogurt retailer with three branches in the San Francisco Bay Area. As with so many customer service–oriented companies, hiring and retaining the right employees are monumental challenges for Fraiche and are among those to which most small business owners easily relate. Across the past 50 years of organizational behavior research, academics and scientists have consistently found that motivational "games" such as Employee of the Month or sales incentives and premiums have effectively spurred on short-term goal achievement. Although somewhat at odds with systems theory and individual goal-setting theory expounded by Douglas Vermeeren and Tony Robbins, who emphasize visualization and personally driven goals, sales incentive programs—and the Funware that is increasingly replacing them—are a multibillion dollar per year industry.

Bitten by the Achievement Bug

Sales teams live to close.

They meet quotas, stretch for deadlines, develop customer relationships, and use the power of persuasion to clear old inventory and draw new products into channels. Given the unique challenges of the profession, most salespeople are likely to be Achievers, and some may be Killers, according to Bartle's typology. These are people persuaded by opportunities to excel and succeed. From a structural standpoint, businesses that ask themselves more than simply "Who was the top salesperson in September?" have the potential to wield great power.

In the fall of 2009, the New York City Health Department made it mandatory for all home care, hospital, and hospice employees to get flu shots in anticipation of the H1N1 flu pandemic. The outcries rang out from the covers of daily news magazines and on network news channels. Not everyone wanted to get a flu shot, and activists raised legal challenges to the state's ability to mandate such an action. Although the decree was ultimately passed, those responsible are still wading through its backlash.

Other health management systems handled matters differently than New York City. For example, Florida's Medicaid Reform program *encouraged* its clients to take an active role in their health by creating a system of credits that are exchangeable for health care items. People who get flu shots, schedule regular visits with their doctors, participate in drug and alcohol abuse prevention programs, and vaccinate their children against disease receive these credits. Consequently, Florida's Medicaid program has seen a substantial increase in flu shots for those individuals who are aware of their involvement in the program. Some districts that use such an incentive structure have reported greater than 80 percent voluntary participation—particularly when time off from work was provided as an incentive—as compared with an anemic 35 percent of younger adults who normally receive the seasonal flu vaccine. Perhaps New York State's health officials would have been equally successful with an incentive structure instead of a mandate. Certainly, happily vaccinated employees would be more willing to recommend the flu shot to recalcitrant patients—and isn't that more important in stopping the pandemic overall?

Similar to New York State, most businesses have quite a bit of leverage when it comes to motivating their employees. Long before an employer threatens dismissal, staff members can be plied with prizes and limitless rewards. Every time business owners want to incentivize behaviors without spending a cent, game mechanics offer ideal methods for their promotion.

One simple game might encourage flu shots by offering employees (or "players") a month's worth of casual Fridays *or* 100 points. In the beginning, the offer of a month's worth of casual Fridays might hold more appeal than points. But what if the players knew that by accruing 1,000 points, they would level up to a status where they win casual Fridays for six months out of the year? If a player understands the game— and plans to still be employed in six months' time—he or she is more likely to bank those 100 points toward goals within the structure of a larger game.

As a method for creating a sense of purpose as well as achieving necessary milestones within business, games are un-paralleled. If getting that flu shot is of ultimate importance, perhaps those players should be given a chance to level up immediately. Given that salespeople are also consumers, Funware-centric approaches seem likely to produce the same results with greater satisfaction and fewer lawsuits. But do they produce loyalty in salespeople?

Mary Kay: Generating Loyalty

The Mary Kay pink Cadillac is one of the most iconic visuals of any sales-based organization. It's also one of the greatest badges offered in sales motivation Funware. For the

1.8 million Mary Kay sales professionals on the front line, getting this car is the ultimate demonstration of their success. Not only is it lavish and meaningful within the organization, it is an unparalleled means of branding for the company. If someone wins a pink Cadillac, everybody—even those outside the Mary Kay community—understands that it is associated with a superior Mary Kay cosmetics salesperson. And since the inception of the famous program in 1968, more than 100,000 top-performing directors and national sales people have earned a company-paid pink Cadillac.

Mary Kay is a brand devoted to rewarding its employees, many of whom peddle their products door to door, throw parties for their friends, and encourage sales through in-person demonstrations. In the design of the Mary Kay program, recruiting other salespeople can be as—or more—important to success than selling product to end users. Therefore, the levels, badges, points, and rewards within the Mary Kay program must have an impact on both internal salespeople and the end users they serve. In fact, Mary Kay's $2.7 billion worldwide empire has been built on nothing short of employee-consumer aligned Funware. Anyone can buy, and anyone can sell. Do it well enough, and you win.

Trust and Motivational Funware

Other than providing tremendous alignment between employee and consumer, consider the message that the Mary Kay pink Cadillac sends to the prospective customer: that the person about to pitch products has successfully sold a large quantity of these products to other and likely similar people. It also puts consumers in close personal alignment with the products themselves. Thus, the Mary Kay Cadillac provides social validation of the rep's supposed knowledge or skill.

In trust-related jobs, badges indicating strong performance levels are universally appreciated by those who see them. City bus drivers who have achieved "safe driver" badges are comforting to riders and encourage them to take more buses. If they were incentivized to do so, cab companies might encourage safe driving by reserving a number of high-visibility cabs for their best and safest drivers. Drivers who met and maintained the safety criteria would be able to drive purple cabs, for example, instead of standard yellow ones. As consumers became aware of the program, they might opt to take the purple cabs over yellow ones. Further, critical "hold points," like hotel and nightclub waiting lines, might naturally prioritize the safe drivers as a service to their customers.

The game might be as simple as formally acknowledging drivers for having zero accidents, complaints, or tickets reported to a more complex series of points garnered through challenges and fare box performance. If the qualifying period was weekly, employers might begin to see their employees fight harder for safer driver practices than for on-road position, thus simultaneously encouraging the taxi agencies themselves to act more responsibly.

But if the game grows repetitive over time, players will likely lose interest and stop playing altogether. In the case of the purple cabs, it might not be a bad idea to create a larger game for the drivers whereby they would be rewarded for both real- and virtual-world accomplishments. By taking tests on road safety, drivers could beef up their points and win that purple cab.

However, offering only one reward would have an effect similar to that of limiting challenges to one type of player. A successful cab program might then add green cabs for environmentally friendly drivers and blue cabs for drivers who passengers have reported as being particularly courteous and helpful.

Of course, if everyone has a purple, green, or blue cab, the game's designers would need to create a level above (platinum, perhaps) to maintain differentiation. But that would be a small price to pay for a city full of courteous, safe, and environmentally conscious cabbies.

As with all Funware designs, the more targeted opportunities there are for players to succeed, the more they will make an effort to win.

Sales Teams and Customer Trust: Pep Boys

One business where trust plays a major role between customers and employees is auto maintenance. Most people don't know the first thing about what keeps their cars running, yet these machines are often sacred members of the family. A lot of people have heard or have professed themselves, "I wouldn't take my car to just *anyone*."

Pep Boys, the largest aftermarket auto maintenance chain in the United States, recently created the simplest of loyalty programs. Customers receive free services over a period of time for continuing to use Pep Boys for their automotive needs. However, if this program became part of a greater online game, the company would be able to powerfully position itself and its mechanics as people their customers could truly trust.

Perhaps the game would have the customer choose a real-life Pep Boys mechanic from the Pep Boys branch they frequent to use as their "mechanic" within the context of the game. Every time a Pep Boys mechanic was chosen by a customer, he or she would receive points. Customers could then earn points by answering questions about car maintenance and upkeep, which mechanics could answer directly. If the mechanic answered questions correctly, both the customer and the mechanic would get points. Of course, points could also be awarded to the mechanic by the customer for courteous service and successful work. Further, mechanics could award points to customers for coming in at the right intervals for oil changes, tire changes or balancing.

As the game progresses, mechanics with the most repeat customers would get bonus points and readily level up while there would be a penalty if a customer switched mechanics. In this way, trust and relationships would be given a Funware boost while aligning the interests of the company, mechanics, and customers around long-term service objectives.

Making the Corporate Personal through Games

Large service-oriented businesses often lack substantial interpersonal relationships between their customer base and their frontline employees. Few people know any of the tellers at their local bank branches anymore. As ATMs and online banking take over from face-to-face interaction, how can banks offer any kind of personal touch?

In the 1980s, Aggie Zichermann was a teller at a branch of the Royal Bank of Canada, then the country's largest financial institution. Zichermann always had a separate line form in front of her station, though there was no incentive for Aggie or her customers to do so. She had developed a clientele over years of working on the bank's front line. Through word-of-mouth networking in the largely immigrant communities around the branch, customers would routinely choose to bank explicitly with her despite the lack of any apparent advantage. Though the branch is still there, the lines at the ATMs have supplanted those at the (now greatly diminished) human tellers. Beyond the special business kiosk, there are no separate queues.

But the demise of personalized banking isn't solely a response to the inexorable march of technology. There never was much incentive for either the teller or the customer to engage in such friendly interactions. When considered through a non-Funware lens, one could be forgiven for concluding that such incentives were unnecessary. Discounts for repeat teller patronage or cash bonuses for seeing more customers are actually counterproductive for banks that attempt to reduce their cost of operations. In a perverse way, financial institutions have an incentive *not* to provide more personal service.

In an online game, however, the cost limitations do not apply, and personal service and customer relationships are eminently viable. Early efforts to integrate the virtual world with the physical world of finance have been largely confined to the realm of experimental marketing. Still, they have yielded interesting results that can be valuable in the construction of a customer service Funware model.

Funware at Work: Wells Fargo's *Stagecoach Island*

In early 2005, Wells Fargo launched a virtual world inside Second Life (since moved to standalone) called *Stagecoach Island*. The idea was to provide a fun hangout for young people that would expose them to the bank's brand and allow them to socialize while encouraging them to learn techniques for sound financial management. Today, *Stagecoach Island* continues to provide such a casual social environment for teens and other Wells Fargo customers. By reimagining *Stagecoach Island* and adding Funware, though, Wells Fargo could blend the real and virtual worlds to produce concrete and meaningful financial results—for itself, its employees, and its customers.

As an example of how today's experience could be improved, *Stagecoach Island* customers could choose a "teller" from either a real-world or virtual bank branch in the form of an avatar. Initially, the customer's choice might simply be based on a bio or a look, though it would be ideal to allow customers to see individual bankers' performance on a leaderboard. Bankers might even offer individual virtual point rewards for choosing to sign up with them.

Once aligned with their personal banker, customers would be given a set of challenges to meet, points to earn, and levels to achieve that would be fun and engaging and would accomplish the bank's objectives (more money under management, more interest-bearing loans to worthy customers, and more timely repayments). As an example, customers might be encouraged to increase their personal savings rate by 10 percent or prepay 1 percent more on their mortgage each month.

In parallel, the tellers would be encouraged to keep up with the game and solicit new customers—because every new customer would help them succeed. Their goals might include developing the biggest following among customers and keeping those customers happy, which could be tracked through the receipt of virtual gifts. To foster goal alignment, these tellers would in effect be on the same team as the customers themselves.

Points would be added to a banker's total when his or her clients save money, and every 10 customers who level up would result in the teller receiving a badge. Therefore, what the customers do with their money would have a direct correlation to the banker's score and create a sense of personal investment. Through the use of a smartly designed and judiciously executed point system, customer data would be kept private while still accomplishing this objective.

The premise here is that the client would choose a teller with whom he or she felt a personal connection. Meanwhile, the teller could be counted on to integrate the client's needs with the bank's objectives as defined through the challenges. No cumbersome manuals or all-hands meetings needed; if the challenge is in the game, it's the company's objective. Relationships could bleed from the virtual to the real world without any limitation, encouraging investment in the bank through trust . . . even if the teller is at a call center in Indiana.

By creating programs filled with challenges and rewards that are symmetrical among customers, the bank, and its representatives, individual play becomes team play. When you have an incentivized employee, you will also have a motivated customer.

Playing Together

Building close relationships between customers and a brand's frontline employees is an obvious challenge. The larger the company, the more likely a personal touch has been placed on the back burner. Instead businesses will choose to message personalization rather than deliver it. With the emphasis on branding and corporate image over customer relationships, even the best-designed marketing campaigns can be dashed on the rocks of poor or indifferent service. Just ask the employees of frequently berated—but well-branded—companies like United Airlines and Sprint. The hangover from poor execution at the front line can be immense.

But Funware provides an answer to this quandary. Instead of merely seeing game mechanics as being an effective tool for motivating sales teams to achieve company goals in a vacuum, Funware can be deployed to align consumer, sales, and corporate objectives into a unified, participatory whole. As any team game-player can tell you, results are best when everyone's on the same page.

But if a challenge could become a longer-term piece of Funware architecture, alliances could be forged. Players and employees could team up. Relationships would form. In an environment where point systems, badges, and levels are creating and maintaining meaningful play, people will continue to engage. By implementing a constant stream of challenges focusing on different motivations and skill sets designed to align everyone instead of merely selling product, businesses can build solid and long-standing customer relationships in perfect harmony with their frontline employees.

Key Concepts:

- Games create a strengthened loyalty among employees.
- Florida's Medicaid program had success getting users to get flu shots by offering credits.

(*continued*)

(continued)

- Employee-consumer aligned Funware helped build the $2.7 billion Mary Kay empire.

- Rewards for safety are powerful tools, especially in transportation businesses.

- By creating team play between frontline employees and customers, each party has a personal investment in the other.

Everyone Wins: Games in Your Business

Product Power

Anyone who has ever watched someone trying to win a giant, leaky Styrofoam ball-stuffed animal at the fairgrounds understands that an impressive prize isn't always necessary to encourage game-play. In fact, a well-designed game can produce substantial psychological rewards simply by tapping into users' intrinsic motivations. Whether they are Achievers, Explorers, Socializers, or Killers, Funware and game-based marketing readily excite today's consumers.

If a consumer is emotionally invested in a brand-centric Funware experience, common practice has shown that he or she is likely to keep playing—even if the underlying product fails to meet expectations. As has been demonstrated with frequent flyers, a well-designed game can make people fly American Airlines simply to maintain their status in AAdvantage—despite the airline's declining service levels. In fact, the vast majority of frequent flyers have fallen victim to the power of a well-designed Funware application, traveling out of the way, overspending, and jeopardizing their relationships in pursuit of some bonus miles.

Behind this slavish devotion to the perks of FFPs lies a disarmingly simple conclusion: game mechanics such as points, badges, rewards, levels, challenges, and leaderboards can be combined to create powerful loyalty tools that can work for any brand. From banking to baking, Funware is taking root as a toolset for savvy marketers looking to break through the *noise* to create enduring loyalty.

But what does the future look like if consumers are more aligned to loyalty programs than to the underlying products themselves?

The marketing dictum that "good marketing cannot compensate for a bad product" is patently turned upside down in the Funware world. Airlines exceed at mediocrity, and yet the most maligned among them use their loyalty programs to keep customers flying. Moreover, as society evolves to become even more game-centric and Generation G rises in importance, consumers will begin to expect rewards for *everything* they do.

Whether your brand is on the leading or trailing edge of this unmistakable gamification trend is up to you, but the outcome is inevitable: everything is about to be made more fun.

But if games and other industries merge, what are the implications? Does Funware portend a future in which game companies will be competing directly against established consumer packaged goods brands for dish soap supremacy? Will Nestle buy the Madden franchise and start promoting football games to sell chocolate?

That seems an unlikely future. But make no mistake: games are competing with advertising for consumer attention, and simply placing ads inside popular titles won't regain your customers' lost affections. Therefore, if you choose to lead the charge headfirst into loyalty, you stand to gain substantial market share over your competitors.

Advergames and In-Game Advertising

With the rise of games and the decline of television as a form of consumer entertainment, savvy marketers have been leveraging two of the best-known and most easily accessible game marketing techniques: "advergames" and in-game advertising.

Advergames are games made explicitly to market a product. The most common examples are small browser-based games that are tied to a specific promotion where typical designs are associated with shallow and quick-play experiences that lack depth and continuity. Conversely, in-game advertising allows brand and product marketers to insert their messages into third-party games, such as a billboard for Michelin tires scrolling past in a mainstream driving game like *Grand Theft Auto*. This category—projected to rise to $2 billion in revenue by 2012—is an important new channel for advertisers seeking to engage with 18–34 year olds outside of television.

Because both categories have established histories of limited efficacy, they offer critical lessons for Funware design. Due to their constrained play offerings and obvious advertising bent, today's advergames are markedly less effective than viral videos or direct promotions for communicating with consumers. The lack of coherent point systems, levels and badges, and engrossing, social play tend to naturally restrict consumer interest.

Similarly, in-game advertising suffers from lack of brand coherence and consumer attention. While racing around a track at 90 simulated miles per hour, a player is highly unlikely to stop the game to respond to a billboard ad. Like the real-world analogue, most in-game advertising provides great air cover to a solid direct marketing campaign.

So, while advergames and in-game advertising offer unique (if relatively weak) value propositions for the savvy marketer, they can be markedly improved with the addition of Funware mechanics. Previously banal advergames can be brightened by stitching their play together with a point system, and in-game ads can be shown as part of challenges linked in a larger Funware environment. The possibilities are endless.

Pursuing, Engaging, and Rewarding Customers: The Business of Lifestyles

Once the dust settles on your game-centric strategy, an interesting (if mildly existential) question may arise: what business are you *really* in?

If you had asked that question of a slide rule manufacturer right before Hewlett-Packard's introduction of the pocket scientific calculator in 1972, what do you imagine that manufacturer would say? Does the fact that we can't name any of those companies—but are very familiar with IBM and HP—tell us something about their "marketing myopia?" In the era of powerful social networks and the rise of games, no company is immune to the need to ask this question—a reality that presents a unique opportunity for marketers. Moreover, this integration of product and the social graph (as in notifications on a person's Facebook Wall) means that product choices have become decidedly public, raising the stakes for every brand.

So, perhaps we are all in the social games business. And that's a good thing because the power of Funware allows marketers to direct user behavior and build loyalty in a way that wasn't possible through traditional advertising. However, if another business establishes a better, more fun offering and continues to produce a good product, customers will inevitably migrate in that direction. In the same way that MySpace lost many active users to Facebook, marketers must continue to reinvigorate their games as well as the products they represent.

Arming Your Business

This book has spent a lot of time asking you to look at your business and assess your marketing expectations and goals. While game-based marketing is on the threshold of inevitability—due largely to the endless march of games as a medium, the ascendancy of Generation G and the lower cost/ higher yield of the Funware approach—it is also another tool within a traditional marketing hierarchy.

Commercials and print ads continue to serve a purpose, and it's important to realize that game-based marketing doesn't require a shift *away* from critical branding and direct promotional strategies. In fact, through the use of a holistic Funware approach, direct and brand advertising can become substantially more effective: users are more likely to opt in, promotions have a given framework, and reward schemes are cheaper. In short, most marketing methods can benefit from a connection to Funware.

First Steps Are the Hardest

Despite the setbacks of many traditional marketing approaches, from the Seinfeld-Microsoft campaign to the decline in brand approval for McDonald's, the future of marketing is extraordinarily bright.

Of course, integrating Funware into the mix may be difficult. The developers of NBC's iCue (described in detail in chapter one) faced some familiar challenges when building its lauded Funware application. iCue combined quizzes, badges, levels, and points with an engaging videoclip-centric game meant to monetize 50-plus years of NBC News archives. Producer Chris Tiné acknowledged that the underlying project at NBC was somewhat of a skunkworks at first, taking place far below the line of senior management. As the project grew into the Facebook success that became iCue, traction was possible only through the dogged support of senior management and the technology teams that worked on it feverishly.

In short, the politics of getting such an innovative project completed at NBC were probably similar to those faced by any game-savvy marketer in a large organization: a copacetic marriage of "under the radar" and heavy artillery support (when needed).

But the successful execution of iCue within the NBC organization does illustrate the enormous potential of Funware to transform organizations. Now, game-centered thinking is bubbling up all over the media conglomerate. NBC has received many plaudits for engaging Funware in its online game, *The Office*, and in the development of the MSNBC *Newsblaster* game, for example.

Do It for the Children

While large organizations may struggle initially to integrate game-centric thinking—despite the obvious rewards and imperatives—their customers rarely suffer the same condition. Today's children do not understand the business model complexities of interweaving entertainment among publishing, television, movies, games, and products. All they want is access to their favorite narratives regardless of context. Jordan Weisman of Smith & Tinker is optimistic. He sees industry changes on the horizon. "You realize," he says, "it just comes down to storytelling. It's going to be cohesive."

Similarly, in marketing—as games and traditional ad campaigns are interwoven to make up one cohesive medium for generating interest in products new and old—the early days of tiptoeing around the subject will come to an end. Game-based marketing will charge ahead with exciting and innovative advancements that will transform the way we think about both products and ourselves.

Funware on the Rise

Everyone loves to play. One of the things marketing with games does very effectively is to combine play with some perhaps *less playful*—or more purpose-driven—activity. Through the very personal sense of accomplishment and self-realization inherent in game-play, businesses that incorporate Funware into their marketing will find they get something that is greater than expected.

The general feedback from companies that are already using games for marketing is overwhelmingly positive. Many—including the examples in this book—have actually discovered that their traditional marketing campaigns suddenly have additional leverage. In fact, effective game-based marketing doesn't merely increase a marketing campaign's value by a few percentage points; it can have a lasting, exponential effect on customer attraction, retention, and satisfaction. At this moment, while the majority of marketing campaigns still do not include games, there is a unique opportunity for companies that seize the Funware mantle. In the medium term, customer connections will rise, and long-range competitive positioning will greatly improve. Moreover, by combining the power of customer-oriented Funware with cooperative games designed to rope in frontline staff as well, campaigns will benefit from an exponential boost in performance.

Trends indicate that the power of games is growing. They continue to become increasingly essential to socialization in our own lives and those of our children as our need for and expectations of play increase. As a brand marketer, you are competing with *games* for attention—full stop. While that presents an obvious and daunting challenge, it also creates a similarly gigantic opportunity. For those innovators who are willing to engage with the Fun Future, the possibilities are limitless. Through the diligent application of points, badges, levels, rewards, and challenges, any brand can deliver extraordinary enjoyment.

Now is as good a time as any to take the first step: get in the game.

REFERENCES

Bhalla, Ajay, 2007.

Branding Strategy Insider. http://www.brandingstrategyinsider
.com/2009/07/recession-decisions-shortterm-gains-and
-brand-damage.html#more (Al Ries, July 30, 2009).

Brandz. http://www.brandz.com/output/brandz-top-100.aspx
(2009).

Centers for Disease Control. http://www.cdc.gov/niosh/topics/
construction.

Consumer Affairs. http://www.consumeraffairs.com/news04/
2005/loyalty_cards.html (Martin H. Bosworth, November
11, 2005).

Customers and Capital. http://www.customersandcapital.com/
book/2008/03/delta-northwest.html (March 9, 2008).

Daedalus Project. http://www.nickyee.com/daedalus (March
9, 2009).

Dinomite. http://dinomite.net/2009/united-states-personal
-savings-rate (Drew Stephens, March 5, 2009)

Edery, David, and Ethan Mollick. *Changing the Game: How
Video Games Are Transforming the Future of Business*. FT
Press, 2008.

Facebook. http://www.facebook.com/press/info.php?statistics.

Forbes. http://www.forbes.com/2008/02/20/service-consumers -retail-biz-cx_tvr_0220service.html (Tom Van Riper, February 20, 2008).

Gamasutra. http://www.gamasutra.com/php-bin/news_index .php?story=24518 (July 29, 2009).

General Accounting Office of the United States. http://www .gao.gov/new.items/d05834t.pdf (July 13, 2005).

Interbrand. http://www.interbrand.com/best_global_brands .aspx?year=2008&langid=1000 (2009).

Kim, Amy Jo. *Community Building on the Web: Secret Strategies for Successful Online Communities* (Peachpit Press, 2000).

Koster, Ralph, and Will Wright. *A Theory of Fun for Game Design.* (Paraglyph Press, 2004.)

Koller, John. Sony. http://blog.us.playstation.com/2009/01/ ps2-sells-over-50-million-units-in-north-america-breaks -console-sales-record (January 15, 2009).

Lampel, Joseph. *Journal of Computer Mediated Communication.* http://jcmc.indiana.edu/vol12/issue2/lampel.html.

Media Buyer/Planner. http://www.mediabuyerplanner.com/ entry/35139/super-bowl-ad-spend-totaled-184b-over-20 -years-rates-quadrupled (January 24, 2008).

North Carolina Division of Pollution Prevention and Environmental Assistance. http://www.p2pays.org/ref/ 19/18713/cpch2.pdf (2002).

Ostrow, Adam. Mashable, http://mashable.com/2009/07/08/ social-media-marketing-growth (July 8, 2009).

Piquepaille, Roland. http://blogs.zdnet.com/emergingtech/ ?p=276 (June 26, 2006).

Preferences for Status: Evidence and Economic Implications. http://papers.ssrn.com/sol3/papers.cfm?abstract_id=1155422 (Heffetz and Frank, 2009).

Sabre Airline Solutions. http://www.scribd.com/doc/6867064/ Frequent-flyer-programs (November 11, 2003).

Sass, Erik. *MediaDailyNews*. http://www.mediapost.com/ publications/index.cfm?fa=Articles.showArticle&art_ aid=108081 (June 16, 2009).

Salen, Katie, and Eric Zimmerman. *Rules of Play: Game Design Fundamentals*. (MIT Press, 2003.)

Schell, Jesse. *The Art of Game Design: A Book of Lenses*. (Morgan Kaufmann, 2008.)

Seeking Alpha. http://seekingalpha.com/article/73934-safeway -stores-incorporated-q1-2008-earnings-call-transcript? page=-1 (April 24, 2008).

Status in Markets. http://www.econ.ucla.edu/zame/Status.pdf (Ball and Eckel, 2001).

Swelblog. http://www.swelblog.com/articles/01-its-airline -deregulation-bday-week-economic-impact-of-com.html (October 20, 2008).

TNS Media Intelligence. http://www.tns-mi.com/news/0313 2007.htm (March 13, 2007).

TNS Media Intelligence. http://www.tns-mi.com/news/0916 2009.htm (September 16, 2009).

TV History. http://www.tvhistory.tv/Annual_TV_Households_ 50-78.JPG.

USA Today. http://content.usatoday.com/communities/ gamehunters/post/2009/08/nielsen-time-spent-playing -games-up/1 (Mike Snyder, August 11, 2009).

Webflyer. http://www.webflyer.com/company/press_room/ facts_and_stats/frequent_flyer_facts.php (Randy Petersen).

Website Optimization. http://www.websiteoptimization.com/ bw/0404 (April 25, 2004).

Wikipedia, United Airlines. http://en.wikipedia.org/wiki/ United_Airlines#Mileage_PlusZDNet.

INDEX